A
PRAYER
THAT
NEVER
FAILS

Dedicated to the infallible wisdom
flowing gently from my guru
Om Swami

A humble offering at his divine feet on his 40th birthday

My guru

I am deep
As I am shallow
Strong as I am weak
Brave as I am afraid
The ebb tide and flood tide
I am the confounding ocean
Its fury and its calm
The dire raging storms.

Unknown to myself
I am much more
When will I seek
If I ever will?
Tomorrow, perhaps
or when death comes knocking
I will die believing
That is all I ever was.

Contents

Herein you will find...

The other side of *sannyasa*

Most people I meet at the ashram, at some point in our conversation, say to me wistfully, 'Life must be so easy for you now that you are a sannyasi.' Or, 'It must feel so wonderful to be free of anger, sadness, hatred, covetousness and envy.'

How I wish! I'm a sannyasi, not a robot.

'You are always smiling because you are steeped in bhakti,' they tell me. 'You are so devoted to God.'

Hmm… if only one could do bhakti 24 hours a day.

'Now that you have donned the ochre robe, you must have vanquished the desires that trouble the rest of us.'

Oh, I have just the odd desire to dazzle devotees with my singing, travel the world with Swamiji or be his model disciple.

These assumptions couldn't be further from the truth.

I first toyed with the idea of writing a book on mental and emotional maladies when I realized how vulnerable I still was to them. Whenever I was in the throes of an emotional upheaval, my ochre robe, my puja (prayer), *japa* (chanting), dhyana (meditation) and positive reinforcement did little to pull me out. It occurred to me then that the old life, with its precarious temperaments and tendencies, which I had discarded in lieu of a life of sainthood, could overpower me as easily as a crocodile clutches and mauls an unsuspecting fawn to death.

The feeling of control that I had rediscovered was but a facade. Like a model patient in a psychic ward who suddenly turns violent and loses months and years of exemplary progress, I too was at the mercy of my untrustworthy mind.

The power of the mind to sanitize useless thoughts, emotions and situations would turn to dust in a matter of minutes. Like a city falls to an invasion, the walls of my mind would lie crumbling on the ground. The cause could be small or big, relevant or irrelevant, rational or irrational, the outcome was always the same—an emotional meltdown of giant proportions.

If only it were severe enough or even lasting enough, I would have learnt to live with it. The tragedy was that it did not seem to have a beginning or an end. Like the deep ocean bed, it had pebbles after pebbles of raw, stale, smelly, prickly and sorrowful emotions that would, all of a sudden, bubble up to the surface. It felt as if these emotions had a sinister presence, lurking like shady mobsters in dark alleyways. They hid themselves well, striking at me when I least expected them.

After three years of deliberate efforts, I still hadn't learnt how to deal with these unannounced intruders. With decisive certainty, they overthrew my caution, wisdom and happiness in the blink of an eye. What wasn't certain, though, was how and when they would strike.

The temporary loss of sanity is, perhaps, far more damaging than a chronic mental condition, for each time it occurs, it strips you of your self-esteem, self-respect, goodness and sense of purpose.

The new life, which had taken me months and years to build, had no meaning in the face of these spells of sadness and madness. That peace and control that I had come to love about my life, was, in reality, at the mercy of angry, restless and negative emotions.

I could still have shied away from penning this book and continued to lead my life as most people do, battling with themselves. However, the throngs of people who come to our ashram to meet my guru, Om Swami, made me realize that I wasn't suffering alone. The world suffered with me. My problem wasn't unique. My failures were everyday failures for others as well. They too were dancing to the fickle tunes of their unanchored, untamed and untrained minds. At one ashram event after another, I have heard countless tales of mental struggles—men and women not knowing what to do with themselves, where to even begin making changes.

On the day of my *sannyasa deeksha*, Swamiji said to me, 'Many people will come to you to share their problems. They will be in pain, in tears even. Be careful of how you use the power the lineage has blessed you with, for a majority out there are suffering because of their beliefs and the poor choices they have made in life.'

I understood the part about poor choices very well; I had made plenty of those myself. But that knowledge didn't lessen my pain or anyone else's. I felt like a headless chicken running on the highway, not knowing what to do, how to begin fixing the big mess called life. And yet, we are all born light and free, carefree as a raindrop cascading from the clouds. It makes no difference to the raindrop whether it lands in a puddle or on lush, green grass; it only knows joy and glee.

My attempts to find a way out of the dark hallways of the mind only became possible by absorbing the teachings of my guru into my everyday life. Swamiji says anything in this world can be learnt, right from music to meditation to being happy and compassionate. One of his foremost teachings on the path of self-mastery, which I have observed from his own conduct, is practice. Practise what you wish to master.

I am reminded of an amusing incident. In 2012, long before I met Swamiji, he had decided not to live his life like a traditional monk, dependent upon the generosity of patrons or donations from devotees. He had been earning his pocket money since he was 9 or 10 years old; there was no reason why he couldn't do it now. 'Donations must go to the causes they are intended for,' he would say, 'and not to my personal needs.'

He chose writing to make a living and share his message with the world. According to him, he wasn't a writer, only a voracious reader. He thought of writing as just another skill that he could acquire with practice. When his first book, *If Truth Be Told: A Monk's Memoir,* was released in December 2014, we went for a multi-city book tour. In one of the metros, the publisher and chief editor of a reputed publishing house came to discuss the possibility of signing him up as an author. The meeting went well, and they seemed quite impressed by Swamiji's depth and breadth of knowledge. At the end of the meeting, I went up to the lift to see them off, and as we waited for the lift, the publisher, a sweet gentleman, asked me in a soft tone, 'Does Swamiji write all his books and blog posts?'

I looked at him in surprise, and then I started laughing. 'Of course, he writes everything by himself, who else would do that? I am just a developmental editor; all I do is suggest a few changes here and there in his manuscripts,' I replied.

'That's truly impressive, because that's not the case with many other gurus,' he said, pleasantly surprised.

In Swamiji's own words, 'The right practice leads to an inevitable expansion of consciousness.' It is a point of no return for the ordinary human mind, from where one's whole existence becomes a prayer. Before we begin, I must tell you though, that behind every prayer there is a story, a horror, a loving or painful cry, a helpless plea. It is never a pretty sight to peel the layers of the human mind, but then, no one said spirituality was easy.

I hope you enjoy reading this work as much as I enjoyed writing it. If you find anything meaningful in it, it is all my guru's grace.

When all else fails

In a world where many religious gurus run huge empires, have a mad following and a madder truth to uphold, Swamiji offered me a simple truth: '*Simplicity of the heart is the seed of happiness.*' How difficult could it possibly be to be simple at heart? I wondered. And yet, just as the morning sun heats up, as the clock hand moves, simplicity of the heart is eclipsed, just like long afternoon shadows darken unkempt verandas.

As a renunciate, I built my new life brick by brick, inch by inch. I began to build a wealth of practical knowledge, an intuitive understanding that came simply by observing Swamiji's unfailing conduct. Just as a loose electricity wire jolts the living daylights out of the unaware passer-by, I was in the proximity of a powerhouse whose might is still hard to fathom.

Yet, with all the success I was achieving in my mantra sadhana, there were times I would completely break down. In my early days as a sannyasi, during peak times for events in the ashram, I would feel like a fraud when I counselled a devotee. It amazed me how I stood there spouting advice to people, while in my private time, I was wrestling with my own demons. But the divine grace was such that the words I uttered out of empathy were of help to some. They would tell me this was exactly what they needed. I even started joking, 'Oh, I don't know my own powers.'

What amazed me most was that if I knew the right things to say and do and it helped people, why was I unable to help myself? Why did all of my high thinking and advice fail when I needed it? I realized then that it was the case with everyone. We all know right from wrong and have the best of intentions. And if not for infrequent lapses in judgement, we would all be saints at heart.

Possessing wisdom or the right knowledge is not the problem; the problem lies in implementation. The mind is not habituated to execute our noble thinking.

Despite the colossal self-doubt, which I hid remarkably well under the garb of a picture-perfect smile, people kept seeking me out.

A vital factor, of course, was that people didn't really have any way of getting in touch with my guru, beyond the brief private meetings that lasted all of three minutes. The next best thing, they figured, was to chew Sadhvi Vrinda's head. (I'm kidding about the chewing part.)

In 2017, my self-esteem was at an all-time high, with all those people bowing and doing *pranams,* not because I had suddenly become a divine being, but because of the great faith they had in my guru. If he had chosen me to be his disciple, there must be something special about me, they thought. Yes, if arrogance and conceit could be considered as special traits, I possessed them alright. So, here I was given the gift of *sannyasa* by none other than Om Swami, and I was still struggling with the same old tendencies of grief, anger, ego and envy.

A year later, when I had mellowed a bit, I asked Swamiji one morning, 'Swamiji, why am I still the same despite all the puja and mantra sadhana? All the praying in the world isn't helping me rise above these emotions. I am sick and tired of myself.' With a grave look, Swamiji said, 'Sadhviji, now you know how I have been putting up with you all these years.'

Swami Vidyananda, who was sitting next to him, laughed uproariously with Swamiji.

This is the most endearing thing about Swamiji. You can be down in the dumps, ready to jump off a cliff, and he will diffuse the situation with humour. With a wan smile on my lips, I pleaded for his help. 'There are many wonderful changes in your behaviour and outlook to life and more will happen, Sadhviji. Inner transformation is a slow process, a painful one too,' he said, encouraging me to look at my achievements in the past year. I asked, 'My mind... the control over my emotional state, I still lose it without any warning. Where am I going wrong?'

'Sadhana, meditation and prayer are not enough to kill these old restive tendencies of the mind.' 'What more can I do?' I asked, resigned. 'Self-purification does not come merely from meditating on and chanting the divine names. Your entire perspective has to change. The change in perspective has to be cultivated methodically, consciously and continuously, until one day, it becomes your second nature. Your mind needs to be reprogrammed to act and think in a certain way.' He asked me to be more compassionate and empathetic. Pointing to my robe, he instructed me to be more mindful and never forget the responsibility that came with the robe.

Time and again, I was baffled by the gradual evolution, for I was indeed slowly beginning to experience the spiritual touch of a sannyasi. On numerous occasions, my intuition worked as if I was reading the future from a book; and at times, it failed miserably, as if I'd accidentally picked up a book of fiction and read it as a reference book. This see-saw of emotions and evolution wasn't exactly comforting, for it lacked any security or constancy.

This everyday struggle of balancing between being a good-natured person, intuitive and capable of certain healing, and being an average human being with the usual challenges, was intolerably frustrating. Increasing my spiritual practices wasn't enough to overcome these challenges. Swamiji gave me my first sadhana in 2013. It has been over six years and I haven't missed a day. Yet, even now, I cannot claim to have tamed my mind. It's a slow battle, as if I were getting the body and mind rid of a cancerous growth. With Swamiji's ceaseless patience, I realized that for the chemotherapy of transformation to work, meditation and chanting weren't enough. I needed a prayerful, practical outlook. I needed an alternate therapy.

The e-mails were still flowing in, paying their respect—*pranams* at my lotus feet. Once, I remember looking at my feet and thinking they were as dirty, cracked and callused as most people's feet. The only lotus feet I knew were my guru's, pink and delicate, and warm with the heat of his *tapas*.

I would repeatedly remind people that I didn't have lotus or divine feet, but they would write it anyway. I didn't know how to tell them that I was just like them, with one great difference—Swamiji's immense grace was upon me. So, notwithstanding my many shortcomings, he blessed me to use all that I had learnt from him to help others. Swamiji often said, 'The biggest strength of our country is the faith people place in this ochre robe. We must never hurt their sentiments andf always act in a manner befitting a renunciate.' My biggest challenge was to quickly become deserving of the pedestal I found myself perched upon. This book is my attempt to capture my guru's teachings and his work with me, in turning me from a hassled, weak and wavering person into a stable and balanced human being.

Whether I have succeeded may never be known because as Swamiji says, 'Self-realization is not an outcome but a journey.' All I can say is that I am trying, and perhaps, my words in these pages may help you the way my master's words helped me.

Book I
Know Yourself

burā jo dekhana maiṃ calā, burā na miliyā koya,
jo dila khojā āpanā, mujhase burā na koya.

I went out looking for a sinner, but I couldn't find any. When I looked within, I found that I was the worst of them all.

—Kabir

Know your mess

Let me tell you a story. It's not the main story, more like a subplot. But it's one hell of a subplot. It's important that I tell this story, not to wash dirty linen in public, but because some truths are best understood when you have been there, done that. Besides, if I don't have the courage to confess my mistakes, how will I ever be who I've set out to be?

In 2011–12, my marriage was all but over. An altercation that had grown violent saw the end of a happy married life, and I came to live with my mother. We were raised in a household where you could get away with anything, as long as you were brave enough to tell the truth and take responsibility for it. My divorce was underway and Mamma, though more anxious than ever, was happy to see me in a new relationship. Life was certainly moving on, maybe not smoothly enough, but there was the promise of new things to come. Mamma was glad to have me home, and happier still that I was well and seeing someone. There was one hitch though—this man was married. I was so blinded by my desire to have a little garden, a dog (one I already had) and a man who came home from work while I sat reading in the house like a memsahib that I chose to get seriously involved. He made some promises and broke some, but every time, I felt he had a valid reason for not keeping his word. His assurance that he would divorce his wife within days stretched to weeks and then months. In time, despite all the promises he kept breaking, I refused to see what everyone around could see all too clearly—that this was a recipe for disaster.

I naively believed that if I was truthful and persevering enough, the situation would work itself out. What I believed to be faith in God was, in reality, plain stupidity, even cleverness on my part. One afternoon, I called up his wife and informed her that her husband was deeply in love with me. You can imagine the chaos that followed—the bitter storm, the crying, the drama, the ugly mess. All through this storm, Mamma stood by me, as did my brother and his wife. (Nobody really had a choice; I was always too strong-headed for them.) Many nights, through the walls of their rooms, they could hear me sobbing, calling him up again and again until the phone's battery ran out or I fell asleep from exhaustion. I think that is why I hate speaking over the phone even now.

Everyone may not relate to this story. Men might find it silly and women may think it was plain idiocy; but among you, there will be one or two people who would have messed up just as foolishly in their lives. Perhaps, to that small minority, this story will make sense.

Anyway, nothing came of my selfish pursuit of happiness. By now, I had little love to give my family, while I continued to feed on their reserves of goodness. The biggest regret I have is for the one time that Mamma spoke to this man over the phone, almost pleading with him to make good on his promise. When he refused to do so, Mamma cursed him as only a mother can. A widow of four years, she worried constantly about what would happen to me after she died. Just how much she worried is a story for another time. In that rage, Mamma had roared, furious as a lioness protecting her cub. After she had hung up, I remember her cradling my head on her chest. There was no chastising, no scolding, no 'You've brought this upon yourself'. She just held me like a mother holds her precious child. Sadly, I was too self-centred back then to feel her love or pain.

Three weeks later came the heart attack. All her worrying, anxiety and emotional upheaval had reduced her heart's working capacity to 40 per cent. When her kidneys failed, I had to take her for dialysis to the hospital thrice a week. I would see the big hole they had made in her jugular and tremble with shame and remorse. To make light of things, I blamed her unhealthy eating habits for landing her in hospital. I reminded her of the bag of chips she had eaten the night before she had the heart attack. I told her that her BP had shot up because of the high sodium content of the chips. 'That's why I tell Sunny (my younger brother) and you not to have junk food. All that oily stuff, Mamma... look what it's done to you.' In her usual gruff manner, she replied, 'Shut up, you know nothing.'

We both knew she was dying because of all that worrying and the high-tension drama in the house. I was responsible for her condition. At 56, when most women are free from all responsibility and have grand plans of spending time with their children and grandchildren, my mother was on a hospital bed, still worrying about what would happen to me after she was gone. Her death was a wake-up call, but even that didn't wake me up completely. It took another three years before I woke up to the reality of my many shortcomings.

I came to realize that small actions have big consequences, consequences that we can't fathom at that time.

Much later, after renouncing the world, I realized how good we are at creating ugly messes in our lives. What we don't know is how to clean up afterwards. No one knows how to clear the mess.

What I really want to say with this story is that we all have big or small messes in our lives—mistakes that dictate, destroy and devour our lives and the lives of those who love us. Should we hold ourselves responsible for these mistakes all our lives? Must we carry these regrets to the grave? Should the ugliness of one aspect of our life blacken the rest of it? Or, will we get up and get back on our feet? I would go with the get-back-on-the-feet option, because that's what I did. In the cool shade of Swamiji's gentle teachings, I found myself taking baby steps towards a brand new life.

It is what made me seek Swamiji out—he didn't care who I was and where I had been, he only saw what I could and would become one day.

A cyclical madness

It is amazing how we are always worried about the same types of issues in our lives. Things change superficially, but inside, we are seething with the same worries and resentments. These festering issues underneath our calm exterior give rise to great moodiness and discontent. Just as an overcast coastal sky can mercilessly ruin a perfectly joyful day, our changing moods make us act and speak in ways that are detrimental to our well-being.

Heated exchanges, arguments and misbehaviour with loved ones, colleagues, bosses, neighbours and strangers is a routine affair for many people. The strife of daily life has become so exhausting that we don't want to just run away from people, we want to run away from ourselves. In the absence of another person, the mind is quite happy to battle ruthlessly with itself. Can we find any joy in life, if we are always at loggerheads with ourselves?

Once, a fellow devotee, let's call her Zara, had a prolonged foot problem. Her foot would hurt at the slightest movement and she could not even walk properly. She neglected the problem for months, and as a result, a regular hairline fracture was becoming a source of chronic pain.

I was friendly with Zara and had come to admire her sharp wit and childlike innocence.

Since we didn't have a hospital near the ashram, I advised her to consult a specialist in Solan. Like most people who come to live on our quiet premises, she was reluctant to leave the ashram. In the olden days, the woman of the house would say that she would leave the house only when her dead body was carried out upon a bier. Most residents of our ashram feel that state of fierce attachment to the ashram. They don't want to leave even for a day, even if it is for something urgent. This was the case with Zara too.

The day came when Zara had a pronounced limp and was in unbearable pain. She could barely walk. All of which I had predicted, by the way. The prediction had been made by the great power of common sense and reasoning.

I had spent time trying to convince Zara to make that much-needed visit to the doctor; I had reasoned with her that it was necessary to do so right away. Two days later, a visiting devotee, a physiotherapist, did have a look at the poor foot, declaring that it needed immediate medical attention. But she didn't take heed. She didn't take my oft-repeated advice too well either. I realized that I was beginning to sound preachy, but it was hard to quell the instinct that she would do permanent damage to her foot.

I also had another solid reason to goad her into seeing a doctor. Those of us who are all by ourselves and don't have caring and nurturing families tend to ignore our well-being.

When I had first begun to live on my own, I remember that I wouldn't eat properly or take care of my health. The days were fine, but the evenings were claustrophobic—the house seemed empty, the kitchen silent and the living-room space dead.

Benoo, my black Labrador, and I would move from one room to another. We weren't just on our own; we also felt quite sorry for ourselves. Benoo had always had the company of four people at home; she missed the other members more than I did. As for me, I truly hated the evenings and the quiet they ushered in.

It was with this sentiment in my heart—that maybe Zara too was not taking care of her health—that I would push her to see a doctor. In my well-intentioned zeal, I must have come across as a little heavy-handed, for after a while, Zara would change her route if she saw me coming towards her to enquire about her foot.

After quite a few postponed and cancelled visits, Zara did see a doctor and the treatment for the hairline fracture began. In due course, I returned to my place in the city, and about four weeks later, I received an e-mail from her. I gathered from that e-mail that the foot had not healed fully, and somehow, I had something to do with it. Here's the e-mail as it is.

Sadhviji, the last time I was a bit flustered because of my foot. Actually, I don't think you remember, but accidentally, while persuading me to visit the doctor, you said that I would not be able to run for the rest of my life if I didn't visit the doctor.

Surprisingly, my foot is still the same and doctors can't do much about it. As your words are always true, my condition reminded me of your words. That upset me, and hence, my weird reactions. I thought it was best to share this than keeping it in my heart.

It's all good now. I have settled with the foot. I don't know what is the reason though. On a lighter note, could it be that curse?

My first reaction on reading the e-mail was amusement, but on reading it a second time, I realized the vulnerable state of mind Zara must have been in. She was a sensitive, caring and intelligent person; yet, all reasoning must have fled, for she had misconstrued the words I had uttered out of care.

It might seem silly that I was being blamed for the foot, but I wasn't surprised. I had fallen in that trap a million times myself. I had blamed enough people for my wrong decisions to know that blaming the world for our problems is easy. It is easy to tell other people that they have let us down, or that it is their fault that our life has turned out in a certain way. We play this blame game more often than we would like to believe. We give into the silliness of blaming others for our woes. These are the stories we tell ourselves to make sense of the world around us.

Depending on which side of the mental spectrum we wake up, we unburden the load of our unhappiness on those who cross our path. Is it any wonder then that the same people and the same issues keep showing up in different clothes throughout our lives? We run in circles, like a madman chasing a stray down the road, without ever realizing that this madness is cyclical. Bent by the weight of our inner turmoil and instability, we are unhappy with the world. We feel that everyone has wronged us and has got the better of us. Really?

On dark, gloomy, rainy days, I remember a single woman once saying, 'It's as if even the weather has betrayed me.' I had laughed at this statement, but in retrospect, it makes so much sense.

When the inner world is shaky, the whole world appears to be your enemy. And sadly, that day will never come when you will vanquish the enemy, because unbeknownst to you, the enemy lives in you. You are at loggerheads with yourself.

If you allow others to be in your head, there will come a time when that is all you will think about, night and day. The quickest way to get past any festering resentment is to remember that you alone are responsible for your mental and physical well-being. Holding other people responsible, even if they are at fault, is only going to muddy your mind.

Here is another incident to give you some perspective. During a winter ashram event, a young woman in her late 20s, tall and shy, had been keenly observing me. I thought that she might want to speak to me, but over the next four days, she made no attempt to approach me. There was this sadness in her eyes that I could not forget. On the last day of the event, after my morning meditation session, she asked me if I had a few minutes to spare. I asked her to meet me outside the temple in an hour.

It was a hot day for a cold winter morning. The big lawn outside the temple was swarming with devotees who were waiting their turn for a personal audience with Swamiji. I, too, wanted to do my *pranams* to Swamiji. It was a regular practice after my *japa*—I would go for his darshan and excitedly share some divine glimpse or experience Sri Hari had given me. On that morning, I was in a rush to tell Swamiji how Sri Hari had appeared in my mind's eye in all His finery. Swamiji would listen to my chatter for a minute and then shoo me out of the meeting room smilingly, saying, 'Now let me get on with my day, Sadhviji; I have to sit here and smile for the next three hours.'

Being around Swamiji is like being around a turbo source of happiness and laughter. He makes everything seem fun and funny. That morning too, I left the meeting room brimming with happiness.

Outside the temple, the girl was waiting for me. After a quick introduction, she said, 'I had a very disturbed childhood. All I remember is my parents fighting and arguing over everything. My father would even hit my mother and me.' She left it there and waited for me to speak.

I was quiet for a moment. I was convinced there was more to her story. By then, I had met not only school-going teens but women well into their 60s who carried their traumatic pasts in their heads, as if it had happened yesterday. I knew that those images from the past haunted this girl's mind too and distracted her from any productive activity. She found it difficult to relate to people and had very few friends. The floodgate of memories, when open, would carry her all the way back into the whirlpool of a disturbing past. It felt terrible to feel what she and so many others had felt. It was like acquiring an ugly burn mark with no way of getting rid of it.

Knowing what I knew, I said to her, 'Please don't relive the past. It's over and done with.'

'My mind keeps playing it like an old tape. I'm sick of wanting to forget it.'

It seems sad, doesn't it, that one's whole life is spent locked in the prison of a horrid childhood? How can one break free of the past? I didn't know; I needed Swamiji's timeless wisdom to guide me, for the number of people who are plagued by abuse is astonishing.

'Swamiji, people lead such sad lives. How do we relieve their suffering?' I asked him at the next available opportunity.

'Sadhviji, life has given them beautiful moments too, but they choose not to look at those,' Swamiji spoke solemnly.

'It's hard to recover from something like this…'

'Agreed. But you can't go on blaming all of life's failures on something that happened when you were a child. At some point, you have to pick yourself up and find the courage to move forward.'

This wisdom became the basis of my firm advice to others—that at some point you have to pull up your socks. The innate resilience that has got you so far needs to be redirected to reshape and remodel your life. This body and mind are withering away every moment; whatever torment we were put through is long over. The mind is clinging to the past as if it was a former lover. Whatever is happening in the now is in your hands. Just as we bury a dead pet and plant a flower on its grave, we need to bury our old memories, wounds and mishaps in the heart of the brown earth and nourish the new seed of willpower and zeal, so that the spring of life can wash away the winter gloom. What have you gained by clinging to those painful memories? Only more pain, I suppose.

It is wiser to throw the coal of forgiveness onto the fire of resentment, so that the fire does not harm anyone. Nobody is scalded, no one is burnt. As the flames of forgiveness rise, the fire of resentment will start to grow cold.

One way to beat this cyclical moodiness is to take the responsibility for your happiness in your own hands. It is one of the most beautiful lessons I have learnt from Swamiji.

With his kind eyes brimming with understanding and care, he said to me one day, *'You alone are responsible for your happiness, Sadhviji. No one is supposed to make you happy or fill your life with joy. That responsibility is solely yours.'*

Grown-ups never do grow up

On some days, I feel as if time is wielding a white dye and colouring our hair. Do you feel that sudden jerk in the back or pain in the knee? Maybe not yet, but it's in the offing. The body is getting old, but the mind remains juvenile forever. At the age of 30, 40, or as others tell me, at 50 or 60 years, our desires, aggressions and transgressions only transmute into something a little more respectable or suited to our age; underneath, they remain the same, slick and sly as ever.

It might seem harsh to say that we never grew up, neither did our parents nor their parents. There's an occasional bright apple here and there, but it certainly does not make up for the whole rotten lot. So, the problem only compounds itself—bad apples mean more bad apples.

In March 2016, we were busy with the edits of Swamiji's book, *The Ancient Science of Mantras*. I live in the city, which is a four-hour drive from the ashram. It is in the quiet surroundings of my tiny flat that I sit down to work. One evening, after my run, I was enjoying the cool breeze drying the sweat on my nape, when I noticed an elderly gentleman in his late 50s walking briskly ahead of me.

His posture was erect and his gait unmistakably that of a retired Army personnel. I was reminded of my father. Had he been alive, and not drinking, perhaps, he too would have gone for a walk in this lovely weather or sat in the balcony drinking tea with my mother. I remembered his smile. The funny faces he made, his jovial nature and how he would make us laugh at the drop of a hat. In 1989, he had left home to serve in Sri Lanka, as part of the Indian Peace Keeping Force (IPKF). I was barely nine years old. I remember that time when almost every other week, an officer was being flown back home in a chopper, in a coffin.

If a week went by without hearing from Papa, we could feel our mother's anxiety in the air. Those were desperate times. Papa even had my mother join Shahnaz Husain's course for aspiring beauticians, so that if he was killed in the line of duty, his young widow would be able to look after herself and the children.

Six years passed, during which my father moved from one terrorist-ridden area to another, mapping the length and breadth of J&K and Punjab. Blood baths, bomb-blasts, massacres, fake encounters, dead terrorists, civilian casualties... he saw them all. He was a brave man who had volunteered to serve his country five years in a row, and that bravery came at a price. Papa had suffered no bodily harm, but he lost his funny streak—that zeal for life that keeps men sane. My father had returned home a different man, and with his new buddy—alcohol.

In a flash, my mind raced back to the winter of 2007. Papa had been battling alcohol addiction for a few years by then. It was only after his retirement that he had agreed to visit a rehabilitation clinic as an outpatient.

His addiction was too severe to be handled with medi-cation. He had to be in rehab for at least three months, the doctor advised us. With my mother's consent, Sunny and I agreed to get him admitted against his will. It was planned that we would get him checked into the rehab facility the next day on the pretext of a routine blood test.

The next morning, I woke up to loud noises coming from my parents' bedroom.

'You'll see me dead if you send me there, Rita.' Papa's voice, filled with rage and helplessness, travelled through the open door. Oh, just another day in our household.

I figured that Mamma had confided our plans to him. A long, tearful scene ensued, where Papa threatened and emotionally blackmailed Mamma and Sunny into believing that this move would cost them his life. I had heard this rant several times in the last decade. It was unbearable for my father to be without his daily fix. He felt such excruciating pain in his body that he would rather kill himself than be without a drink. My mother was a courageous woman, who had done everything she could to give us a normal childhood.

As always, Papa's pleading and emotional blackmail got to her and she gave in; and my brother followed suit. Suddenly, I stood alone. All the running around to the hospital, planning his recovery and treatment—everything just went out of the window.

Only a few nights ago, Papa, with his frail and bony arms around me, had wailed like a child to be freed of this sickening addiction; he had begged me to help him. I could barely control my tears at his vulnerability. We were both long past the stage of believing that he would ever be free.

Yet, when he had agreed to visit the rehab and Mamma had given her agreement to get him admitted without his consent, hope had soared in my heart. Once again, we were back to zilch. I remember shouting at the top of my lungs at Mamma and Sunny to not listen to Papa, to let me call the ambulance to take him away. All she had to do was sign a consent form as his spouse. But the teams had changed; no one was willing to take that one step that would put him away for three months. What if he hanged himself there as he had threatened to do? Mamma was worried what the relatives would say if that happened. My younger brother was a level-headed person, who had dealt with my father's illness for much longer and far more graciously than I had, but he wasn't willing to go against our mother's wishes either.

Standing in our garden, crying and screaming at the same time, I had begged, pleaded and cajoled, but to no avail. I was 27 years old at that time, screaming on an open lawn next to the road.

'He's going to die, is that what both of you want?' I had shouted at my mother and my brother. No one had answered.

I had felt so helpless, hopeless and alone. If only someone would help me get him to the hospital. Was I the only one who could visualize our bleak future?

In the spring of 2009, less than 18 months later, Papa was due for his regular Military Hospital (MH) visit and yearly check-up. Both my brother and I were home for a brief holiday, when Papa asked me to pack a small bag with some clothes.

'Pack me a bag with two shirts and a pyjama. I might get admitted,' Papa had said, not looking at me.

'Get admitted in the hospital?' I looked at him in surprise, and then my eyes welled up on their own.

I knew he wasn't coming back, otherwise he wouldn't have checked himself in. The doctor told us that a cancerous growth had metastasized in his body. Papa had known this all along. The tumorous growth actually protruded out of the region just above his abdomen, and it was in the final stage. He had been keeping this news to himself for six months. The pain was unbearable now, so he couldn't go without proper medical care. Hence, the decision to get admitted.

You may wonder how his family, his wife and children, could not know that he was suffering from a terminal disease? The truth is that Papa had lived a diseased life for so long—falling, waking up on the floor, being delirious, bleary-eyed and in pain because of too much alcohol (and other things I'd rather not say)—that we could not tell the difference. On the 15th day in the hospital, he passed away.

That evening, while easing into a walking pace, all these memories gushed into my mind. With a pained heart, I wondered where Papa would be today had he met someone like my guru. Swamiji would have shown him the way out. Papa too could have lived a normal life as most 60-year-old retirees do. I felt a sharp and tangible pain at the loss of a good life—a life that had gone to waste because there was no one to steer him in the right direction.

Papa was a beautiful person, kind and generous. From him I had learnt to always stand up for people whose station in life wasn't the same as ours.

'Everyone can say no to their subordinates, but very few have the balls to say no to their bosses,' he would say.

There had been times when his military vehicle had barely missed a landmine. He had always chosen to travel first rather than sacrifice his soldiers to safeguard himself.

Papa was a very brave man. But his struggle with alcoholism, which began during the many years he served in a militancy-ridden environment, all but consumed him.

When we were invited to parties or dinners at other officers' homes, when Papa would get tipsy after a few drinks, both Sunny and I would feel embarrassed. We would be really mad at him when we got home, that is, if Mamma hadn't already started shouting at him. But it's also true that when someone ignored Papa or misbehaved with him, we felt equally resentful of that person, for he didn't really know our father and what a fine-spirited, helpful man he had always been.

Look at me, Papa, see what a beautiful life I have now.... I wish you could have met Swamiji while you were alive. You would have loved him. He would have saved you just as he saved me.

I blinked back hot tears at these strangely soothing memories. I returned home in that sombre mood and pushed these feelings to the back of my mind. A sannyasi is without ties, I told myself. The same night, Swamiji sent me an e-mail regarding some edits of *The Ancient Science of Mantras.*

What he wrote in the second half of the e-mail took my breath away. 'On an unrelated topic, had I met your father earlier, I would have helped him overcome his addiction. I certainly would not have let him go like that.'

The authority in those words, the conviction with which they were written, made me cry. Was there no end to his might and kindness? He was everywhere. I had long ago stopped being surprised at Swamiji's ability to access my past memories or life. In that moment, it occurred to me that if only my parents had had that mental and spiritual support, I would have had a better chance of getting my act together. In the absence of a stable family environment, I had been running from pillar to post all my life.

I wonder if parents realize what a grave responsibility it is to provide their children with a wholesome, happy and loving environment. Becoming a parent is not really based on any system of merit, is it? It's simple biology. But before you decide to bring a new life into this world, you must be sorted, stable and wise enough to raise children; else, it is just kick-starting a circle of disappointment and failure all over again.

You see couples all around, desperate to have children, filled with despair at the thought of living a childless life, and yet, these are the same people who bicker, lie, cheat, squabble and fight every day. What goes on behind the four walls of a home in a seemingly happy family is anyone's guess.

It is saddening indeed that unknowingly, parents set their children up for a life of misery and unhappiness. What is even more saddening is that one day, we too become like our parents, just as vulnerable and flawed.

It is a vicious circle. In failing to grow up, we not only fail ourselves, we fail the generation that succeeds us. A legacy of instability and immaturity gives birth to fickle minds that never grow up. Are you too a grown-up who has never actually grown up? The answer to that is probably 'yes'.

One day, I was trying to pass the buck of my failures and flaws to my parents, when Swamiji pointed out, 'Your parents were good people. They gave you a lovely childhood, with all the comforts and care possible. They had their own set of challenges, and with that, they did the best they could.'

'Swamiji, that is true. But my mind resents the later years. They had become different people; I didn't recognize them anymore. The past is hard to forget. I would have had a better chance at life if they were like other normal couples.'

'What about the present, Sadhviji?' he asked. 'No one is stopping you from living a full life now.'

It is a beautiful perspective. No one was holding me back now. Physically, I was free as a bird. I was not answerable or accountable to anyone; yet, my mind was far from free. It dwelled too much in the past or hankered after a future.

Do you also spend too much time blaming your parents, circumstances and missed opportunities for leading an average life, hiding behind their follies like a coward? Do you?

It is true that every grown-up is a child, behaving and acting like a child. Unless we are sorted in our heads, our mental and emotional upheavals will spill into the lives of the successive generations. Unknowingly, unwittingly, we are creating the world we fear.

When we grow, our families, our friends, the world at large grows with us. We must grow up, so that we may positively impact the lives of those who look upon us for care, protection and learning.

The enemy we love

What do you think the title of this chapter refers to? Take three guesses. Anger? Jealousy? Greed? Lust? No, we are sleeping with a much more powerful enemy, who raids our subconscious and destroys our dreams. It slowly trashes all the precious stuff we own, turning our gold and silver into useless trinkets, and our small wealth of virtues into currency gone out of circulation.

Self-doubt is the enemy we love.

Self-loathing or self-doubt is like a having a shoe-bite every time you wear your shoes. Whenever you decide to walk a new path, start a new adventure, break the old pattern to embrace a new life, the mind starts throwing these poisoned darts of doubts at you. The more you doubt yourself and your intentions, the weaker you become. It is as if the mind enjoys being self-destructive. It cannot stand the thought of abandoning its negativity, its drama. It thrives on unrest and feels threatened in the face of peace and bliss. Sometimes, self-doubt takes on the guise of boredom or shows up in the guise of guilt if you fall for the slightest overindulgence.

In 2017, Swamiji was in strict solitude in the ashram. For five long months, from May to September, he remained indoors in his cottage. He saw no one, spoke to no one and had the luxury of silence seven years after his return from the Himalayas. He was so joyful about disappearing for a few months, living in quietude, in dhyana of the Mother

Divine. It was no surprise that at the end of his five-month solitude, his face glowed like a burning ember. He looked every bit as radiant as the Divine Mother.

During his solitude, Swami Vidyananda and I had the *seva* (service) of cooking lunch for him. We would leave the food tray on the ground floor of his cottage every day at 11.30 am. Free for the rest of the day, I would spend my time in the temple, singing bhajans or writing poetry for Sri Hari. The life-sized *vigraha* seemed to enjoy my company too. It would not be too much of a stretch to say that we had eyes only for each other. I was spending nearly six hours a day in *Bhagwan's* loving company. With rain falling melodiously on the tin roof above, it felt as if a little piece of heaven had come upon earth. There were only seven residents in the ashram during that period.

The monsoon had arrived and outside the temple the sky thundered and raged. River Giri flooded. Every tree, every leaf and every mountain was coloured fresh green. I rejoiced in Nature's lap, serving my guru, singing bhajans, writing poetry and doing my sadhana. Sometimes, it was hard to believe that my life had taken such an amazing turn. I, who had never really knelt down to pray, was leading a life of faith and meaning. It was hard to believe that I was a sannyasi.

Sunny has a great sense of humour. He had joked once, when I had first shared the news of shifting to the ashram, *'Nau sau chuhe khake billi haj ko chali.'* (After eating 900 rats, the cat is going on a pilgrimage.) It was an apt phrase for me; a city cat had come on a pilgrimage to the ashram in 2013 and had stayed back to chant the holy names forever.

Lying in my bed at night, I often wondered why I had this grace. Why now? Did I even deserve it? Was I really any different from the time I had started? My flaws were still there. Like a packet of frozen peas taken out of the refrigerator, I had thawed a little, mellowed, but the rest of me was the same. My memory, like a dog fetching a bone, would then be quick to recall scenes and incidents from the past, disturbing my peace of mind.

At times, memories of incidents long forgotten or suppressed would resurface, and the fear of history repeating itself would reduce my mental state to that of a five-year-old, unsure and uncertain of everything. In a matter of hours, I would switch from being a balanced, stable individual to being volatile and on the edge, like a naked electric wire. I would feel as if time was running out. I dreaded in those moments that someday, I would die with all these regrets and these great struggles with myself left unresolved, and my life could then never be undone.

Just like that, the great ease that I felt with my new life would evaporate and the dark clouds of self-doubt would blow in, and my life would appear to be a facade. I would feel that I wasn't really who I projected myself to be. And I would kneel by Sri Hari's side, wailing like a banshee. In one such moment, trapped in the temple with Sri Hari because of incessant rain, I wrote this poem. It was the first time it occurred to me that perhaps my own mental struggles could help people like me, that maybe I could write a book for the lost and the doubting.

When prayer fails
In that long, dark and lonely night
Just as a dim lantern runs out of oil
The heart burns a slow, painful death.
From that dying flame burst forth
smouldering embers of ego and rage.

Oh, these shadow demons of
menacing heights
then stomp into my anxious mind
a deluge of thoughts
unwanted, unwelcome
muddy the river right running wide.

Oh, how the struggling
consciousness
bravely fights to stay afloat
and yet the choppy waters
turn tail
roaring into a maddening storm.

These episodes of self-doubt and self-loathing would greatly disturb my mental equilibrium, compelling me to lash out at the smiling, black stone idol like an angry child.

Sometimes, my ire would be so strong that I would stop going to the temple.

What was funny was that I would gain back my mental stability just as easily as I had lost it. Like a child who knows she has made a mistake, I would enter the sanctum sanctorum smiling bashfully and seek Sri Hari's forgiveness. Swamiji in all his kindness had accepted me as his disciple, but mentally, I was far away from honouring the ochre robe. My mind was caught between the walls of self-doubt, guilt and failure. It was like a circus monkey had been let loose in a divine dwelling.

One morning in August 2017, I decided that I would not seek Sri Hari's blessings until I was purified in the heart and mind. I vowed that I would not touch the idol's divine, blessed feet until the idol itself asked me to do so. Even if it took me years to purify myself, I would not touch the idol's feet with my grimy hands.

From that day on, I would not go near the idol except when it was my turn to do the *arti*. I told no one of my vow, but I was reminded of it every time other sannyasis sought *Bhagwan's* blessing by touching His feet. Deep in my heart, I hoped that someday Sri Hari would purify me.

However, for all the faith I had in the powers of the *vigraha*, sometimes I would think, 'How could an idol ask me to touch its feet?' It seemed near impossible, but I was okay with it. I had no business asking for things I didn't deserve. I was quick to adapt to the vow and soon fell into the practice of bowing to the Lord from far and not touching His *vigraha*. It became a habit, and soon, I forgot all about why I had adopted it in the first place (typical of me, raging one day, raising a hue and cry and then waking up the next day, marvelling at the beauty around me as if nothing had happened).

On February 13, 2018, just five months later, there was a grand *abhishekam* to celebrate Mahashivaratri. We had just returned from the Bangalore Gayatri Sadhana retreat. Swamiji himself was going to perform the *abhishekam* that day. Five minutes into the ceremony, Swamiji turned to me.

'Sadhviji...' He held a small silver pot filled with water. He beckoned me to pour a little water at the *vigraha's* feet.

Not to keep Swamiji waiting, I quickly did as he asked. I poured the water from the pot at Sri Hari's feet, watching it fall little by little. The *vigraha* stood proud and tall, magnanimous, grandiose, the Master of the Universe. Swamiji then called Shamta Ma and other sannyasis to pour water at *Bhagwan's* feet and the *abhishekam* resumed. When Ma and I took our seats on the floor, I briefly wondered why Swamiji had called me first. In the last four years, I had never seen Swamiji summon anyone to offer water at *Bhagwan's* feet during the *abhishekam*. He always did it himself, and any offering made to *Bhagwan* by sannyasis always followed a hierarchy. What was special about today? Why did he call me first?

Swamiji then smeared ash on the *vigraha* of Sri Hari, covering every nook and corner with the grey dust, which rose like smoke in the air. *Bhagwan's* lotus eyes had become even larger as they shone with the powerful residue. Ensconced in both ash and turmeric, the *vigraha* had acquired a different form. One rudraksha bead was wound after the other until hundreds of rudraksha beads were draped all over Sri Hari. He looked every bit the great destroyer, the ash-smeared Shiva of Mount Kailasha. Gone was the soft playful demeanour of Narayana; in its place was Rudra, the wrathful Lord Shiva.

Swamiji then turned to look at us, his eyes red as vermillion and droplets of sweat trickling down his cheeks. The Rudra *abhishekam* lasted for more than 30 minutes. The energy in the *garbh-gruha* was so tangible that despite the freezing cold, it looked like Swamiji had just finished a marathon. A chill ran down my spine as Swamiji said, '*Har Har Mahadev.*'

The next morning, I reached the temple just in time for the 7 am *arti*. As I entered the *garbh-gruha*, I did my *pranams* to Sri Hari, touched His feet and quickly took my place as Swami Raghavananda blew the conch and the *arti* began. After the morning discourse, when I went to seek Swamiji's darshan in the meeting room, he said to me, 'Wasn't it lovely how Sri Hari let you pour water on His feet during the *abhishekam*, Sadhviji?'

'But why, Swamiji? Why did you ask me to make that offering? It was so different...'

'It is what Sri Hari wished.'

In that moment, I remembered the vow I had taken about not touching *Bhagwan's* feet until He beckoned me to do so. This morning's scene flashed before my eyes—without thinking, I had touched *Bhagwan's* feet, and it had felt so natural. As if by magic, I had forgotten all about my inhibitions of touching Him with my tainted hands. He had indeed asked me to touch His feet.

My eyes welled up in wonder and awe at the benevolence of Sri Hari. With all my flaws and impurities, in His eyes, I was pure. He didn't mind playing my silly games or answering my prayer. I decided then to do away with regret, guilt and the likes of them. If I was pure enough for *Bhagwan*, then I was pure enough for myself, for the world.

Doubting myself and feeling guilty was like digging my own grave. By entertaining thoughts of worthlessness, I was weakening my own roots. I didn't need more enemies on this path to the Divine; I needed to be my own friend, my own staunch supporter, admirer and advocate.

The road that leads to Him is filled with perils and failures. On some days, all that darkness and sadness breaks my will to carry on, and on other days, I can't wait for my day to begin, to offer my humble prayers at His divine feet. This precarious balancing of the two facets of the same consciousness, to me, is life.

Biology of a woman

Are you wondering why this chapter refers to the biology of a woman and not the biology of a man? Well, there's no more to the biology of a man other than the fact that he is genetically geared to procreate, to play around. I mean no offence to the other sex, but the male, once he is well into his teens, realizes that he has little to fear. Nature has equipped him with physical strength and a natural freedom with regard to his sexuality. The problem arises when a girl wades into the deep waters of womanhood.

Confusion, like smoke from a chugging train, rises and clogs the windows of her mind. She carries this confusion into her college, workplace, and surprisingly, to her marriage as well, long after she has become the mother of grown-up kids.

There is a lovely joke that Swamiji once cracked amidst a small group of people, which is so apt here. It was something like this.

'A woman, the mother of eight children, is speaking to her friends about love when she looks heavenwards and complains to the Lord, *"Ya allah, saccha pyar nahin mila"* (O God, I never did find true love).'

Women and their vain quest for true love never really ends. Regardless of whether their partners are the most loving or the most abusive, most women feel something is missing. That 'something', in due course, either turns into 'someone' or a simmering emptiness that grows into a quiet depression. All that an unhappy woman needs is a bit of loving attention and care, and she is willing to change the course of her whole life to chase this elusive togetherness. This constant need for attention and approval tends to weaken the inherent strength and resilience Nature has blessed women with.

I'm not suggesting that women lack the intelligence to make sound decisions or judgements (I'm a woman and I stand for equality). On the contrary, it is their innate sensitivity to people, surroundings and their own emotions that makes them seek a fulfilling life. They realize pretty early that a loveless life is not much of a life. If you disagree with me, imagine what your life would be if you stripped it of your most meaningful relationships.

For whom would you save all the money in those investments and FDs? With whom would you share the joy of your new car, a promotion at work or something as simple as a quiet dinner?

On a business trip abroad or backpacking through Europe, holidaying with strangers might feel exciting, but when the excitement dies down, you want to come home. Home is where love resides, in the eyes of a parent, in the arms of a little one, in the warm kiss of a loving partner.

A very courageous devotee, with a doctorate in mathematics, shared this beautiful story with me. She hasn't asked me to change her name; nor is she reluctant to share the truth as it is. Her story is the story of numerous bright women, who are stifled, suffocated and locked in a prison of society's making. Here is Raina's account in her own words.

My father was a senior bank officer, much respected and loved in our town. I always wanted to become a college professor. My home had an academic environment, where emphasis was laid on good education. My father was a great supporter of education but had a strict stance when it came to matters of the heart. I was a bright, hardworking student and an obedient daughter. In my heart, I had many questions about life and my future, but my parents were disciplinarians and I could never muster the courage to question, oppose or break any rules laid by them. My father had a 12-bore rifle at home, and he would often say that if my sisters or I attempted to have any torrid love affair, he would shoot us himself. We believed it to be true.

Like any other young woman, I longed for love and affection. I was certain that I would love my future husband so much that he would have no choice but to love me just as deeply. I didn't know much about the ways of the world back then. I was only 21, appearing for my final year of Master's in mathematics, when I was married off to a suitable boy, a police officer. I had only spoken to him for 10 minutes a month before my wedding.

By the time I turned 25, I was the mother of two adorable children. My married life was nothing to write home about, but it wasn't bad either. My husband was a decent man. He had a big ego, but that didn't stop him from allowing me to resume my studies eight years after our marriage. There was just one condition though—that the household chores must not suffer on account of my going back to college.

A few more years rolled by. I performed very well academically, and with the encouragement received at college, I got my M.Ed. (Master of Education) degree.

At home, things were the same—a loveless, automated living, where my husband rarely displayed any affection or care. He never abused me physically, but verbal abuse was common. He would repeatedly say, 'You are ugly, but that's one compromise I was willing to make. I didn't want to marry a beautiful girl. I didn't want the additional headache of worrying that my wife might be cheating on me while I am at work.'

There were a hundred innocuous things he would hurt me with.

'Stop slamming the fridge door so hard; your parents didn't buy it for us,' or 'You are getting free meals; that's why you idle away your time on studies.'

After so many years of marriage, I was accustomed to these barbs, and they didn't bother me as much. I was having a good time in college, and my kids were growing up fast. I loved watching them grow, learning new things every day. But a deep void, a longing for love, remained buried underneath the facade of my family life.

I started my PhD in education. I had made my peace with the way life was and didn't really need or want anything more, or so I thought. I had been married for 16 years by then.

When I was close to completing my PhD, life took a strange turn. My husband got posted to a different city, where I soon met an old neighbour. I was delighted to see him, and we exchanged phone numbers. My afternoons were free, and he would often call to catch up. Since he was a school friend too, it seemed natural to talk for hours together; we had common interests while growing up. As is the nature of such relationships, things began to change, and all the desires that lay dormant in my heart burst forth.

I started to distance myself from my husband and started meeting this friend. This went on for six months. On the one hand, I felt guilty, and on the other, I couldn't find the courage to end my new relationship.

One day, when guilt got the better of me, I confessed everything to my husband. He didn't react, almost as if he was waiting all along for an excuse to end the marriage. He simply asked me for a divorce. My friend tried to dissuade me from leaving my husband, but my husband no longer wanted me in his home. I didn't know what to do, as suddenly, no one wanted to have anything to do with me.

My friend then came up with the idea that we would rent a house, where we could live together with my children. He said he wouldn't divorce his wife, but he would live with me. I tried to seek help from my husband, pleading with him to forgive me, to let me stay with him, if not as a wife, then at least as a caretaker for his home and children. I told him that I would never ask him for money. I would earn and support myself, and he was free to do whatever he was doing anyway. But my husband was adamant about getting a divorce. It was a very bad time. I didn't know whom to turn to.

If that wasn't enough, my husband made my life a living nightmare. He told anyone who would care to listen that his wife had been having a sleazy love affair. He spared no one—my relatives, my PhD guide, my father's friends, my friends, our neighbours.... He began harassing me at home, monitoring my phone calls, trashing my documents, until one day, I took my children and went to live with the other man.

It was the biggest blunder of my life. Belatedly, I realized that all doors were now closed to me. My husband sent me two legal notices, one for the children's custody and another for adultery. I had become so depressed that I contemplated committing suicide. There was little left of my self-respect, as if someone had taken pieces of my clothing and hung them out to dry, leaving me with nothing to cover myself.

The thought that I had ruined my children's lives plagued me all the time. I had to end my misery. But who would look after them after I was gone? My mother was a widow now (my father had died of cancer). In these trying times, my sisters and my brother stood by me. Their reassuring words that it wasn't really my fault and that I had to pull myself together for my children's sake, drilled some sense into me. The unconditional love and support of my mother and my siblings restored my sanity. But they were far away in the US, while I lived in India, alone, lost and stranded with two children.

Gradually, I gained some strength and got rid of the spineless man who had led me down this reckless path. Then I gathered all my courage and went to see a psychiatrist. He told me that although I had lost my home, I had what I needed to start again—my PhD, my children, my intelligence. He encouraged me to rebuild my life, to start all over again.

I was on medication for six months.

In time, I started reading spiritual and self-help books, filling my mind with positivity. In March 2015, I came across Swamiji's memoir, *If Truth Be Told*, and it gave me a new direction in life. It was then that things truly started to change. I had his first darshan in May 2015, and in my heart, I immediately accepted him as my guru, the one who led me from darkness to light. With his immense grace and blessings, my sister's unwavering persistence and a PhD in mathematics, I landed a job in the US.

The move to another country did us good. My kids soon settled into the routine of a new life. With faith and resolve, life became truly fulfilling. Today, I am a self-sufficient, independent woman and a good mother. I am there for my children, as my own family was there for me during that awful time. I had many learnings over the years but none as strong as this:

'If you keep walking with courage and strength, the universe works with you and for you. My search for love ended in infinite divine love.'

Somewhere, the young Raina's desires are hardwired in every woman's head. If she isn't in love, then she isn't complete. Love is the oasis that a woman keeps looking for throughout her life. Each sighting of an oasis ends up as nothing more than a mirage. Like the promised land to the Jews, she hankers after the stability, security and sweetness of being in love. You take love out of the equation, and you have a potentially depressed society of women who do not know what to do with themselves. This might seem harsh, and some women might even scoff at it, but it is the plain truth. Nature has created us to nurture, to shower care and affection and receive them in return.

I remember a time not so long ago, when I only saw lost people wherever I looked. Let's envision for a moment that you are standing in the middle of a street. You see people— some familiar, some unknown—going about their chores. They appear strong and capable, and you feel someone among them will surely be able to point you in the right direction, hold your hand and pull you out of whatever problem you find yourself in. But as you approach them, they begin speaking, and the truth about their lives starts falling out like dirty clothes from a crammed closet. These people could be anyone—family members, partners, parents, colleagues, friends or grown-up children. Imagine waking up to the reality that all you are surrounded by is a sea of lost people.

At the ripe age of 32, when I first realized that everyone is lost, I was heartbroken. As long as there was hope that someday happiness would come in the guise of love, I was reassured. But to have figured out that every single person I knew was lost and struggling was a big blow. I had felt helpless numerous times before, but this was a new low of helplessness. It was as if I was surrounded by small boats, all lost at sea. With no one to show the way and a storm building on the horizon, where could I go, to whom could I appeal for help?

The knowledge that no one is there for you is the hardest thing to accept at first.

However, this brutal let-down is the first step. When you start accepting that you have only yourself to rely on, things start moving pretty quickly. Hope, zeal and enthusiasm become regular visitors, propelling you to new, unexplored shores. Raina's story is filled with nerve, grit and a childlike faith that all is set right when you move with courage and belief.

In the ashram, I meet hordes of people struggling to make sense of their relationships. These people comprise confused college-going students, doctors with well-established practices, working women, defence personnel, lawyers, well-to-do-professionals, retirees and people with advanced degrees and skill sets. It might seem like a small sample of people, but it is quite a valid representation of the whole. The see-saw of emotions, constant tug of war, fights and excessive drama in their relationships seem unmanageable and unnecessary, but people don't know how to free themselves. A great sense of non-fulfilment plagues them. A common question is, 'Why is it so difficult to find love and be loved in return?'

In 2012, long before I had even met Swamiji, he had written this beautiful e-mail addressing the turmoil going on in my life at that time. He wrote:

Wherever you are in life, just be there. Don't chase anyone or anything; don't run after love. If you keep doing what you do with sincerity and hard work, love will find you. It'll come to you.

All of his words came true. Today, there is so much happiness, inner joy and love in my life. I practise many creative pursuits such as music, writing, serving others and living a meaningful life under the kind shade of my master. What's more, the love I have in my life now can never fade away; it is not transactional. It is the love of God. Swamiji has led me to Sri Hari.

I long to play in their beautiful yard one day. To be lifted high above this suffering earth and be released into the sky that beholds the glorious form of Narayana, the Supreme Deity, and Mahalaxmi, the Divine Mother. This body that binds me, and the mind that ensnares me, must be cast aside. I have to travel far, to see my eternal Father and Mother. That is my truth.

An underrated spirituality

One morning in 2013, four years after my father's demise, I woke up to lovely Pune weather, windy and cool. The windchimes in the balcony chimed like love birds. Mamma had always loved their gentle tinkling through the day. With a glass of warm water in my hand, I made my way to Mamma's room and plonked myself down on a chair. She sat on the bed, sipping her morning tea and eating Marie biscuits, giving a piece to Benoo every now and then.

As soon as I said, 'Good morning, did you sleep well?', Mamma began to excitedly tell me about her early-morning dream, as if she had just been waiting for one of us to walk in.

'I dreamt of Papa. He told me, "Come Rita, it's time to go'," she told me excitedly, as if it was a holiday invitation and not a premonition of her death.

'Rubbish,' I retorted.

'No *beta*, I also saw doctors in white coats. There was a lot of activity around me. Maybe Papa had come to prepare me...'

'So, did Papa come as himself or as a bird or something?' Sunny piped in from the living room.

He walked in with his drawing board. My brother had this unfailing routine of practising how to draw nude sketches the moment he woke up. (Artists, I tell you!) It was his daily ritual to practise sitting next to Mamma before he left for work. He was now a creative director with an animation company.

His remark referred to a little incident a few days ago. Each morning, at least a hundred pigeons waited for Mamma to give them their morning meal of bajra. A few days ago, a crow had come too and had started cawing loudly, scaring away the pigeons. When Mamma tried to shoo it away, it just cawed louder.

When the crow appeared regularly at the same time for four days in a row, Mamma said to us quite seriously, 'Who knows, it might be Papa who has been reborn as a crow.' Sunny and I had laughed so hard. Only Hindu mothers can come up with this weirdly hilarious stuff! Or who knows, we may have been in the wrong.

So, that morning, as Mamma narrated her dream, the crow started cawing again, but this time, he had brought company—there was another crow with it.

My brother said to Mamma, 'Look, Mamma, today there are two of them. Papa has come with his girlfriend!' Mamma had lovingly whacked Sunny on the head, and there was more morning laughter.

Three days later, a perfectly healthy Mamma had a heart attack. True to her dream, there were doctors all around her, as they took one ECG after another to determine the damage the heart had suffered and its impact on her kidneys and other organs. Seven ECGs later, Papa's warning had indeed come true. Would you call it a coincidence that the dream had played out exactly the same way in real life?

As children, we have all seen some form of worship in our homes—in front of an altar, a picture, an idol or idols—

depending upon our faith and religion. For some of us, this faith matures with age into a deep bond with God; but for most of us, it remains an item to be ticked off in our daily routine. After a bath, fold your hands, light a lamp, recite a prayer and be done with it. As an adult, you might even do away with any form of worship because of dearth of time or lack of belief. As Ghalib said, '*Jannat ki haqeeqat to hum bhi jaante hain Ghalib, par dil behlaane ke liye khayal acha hai.*' (I know the truth of heaven, Ghalib, but at least it keeps the mind entertained.) A life without belief in a higher power or divine force, however, eventually turns into a hollow existence.

Swamiji would always say, 'Spirituality is the anchor that keeps you rooted when the howling gale of chance turns your life upside down.'

It wasn't that I did not know right from wrong when I made disastrous choices in life; it was just that my faith in myself had become so weak that I believed I needed to safeguard my own interests before others' interests.

Had I remained in touch with the strength and resilience within, that inner voice, the voice of the soul would have anchored me. This is what spirituality does, it anchors you. It gives you roots.

Parents, siblings or partners may die or change with time; situations at work or home may change; but your beliefs won't change so easily. I read a beautiful story in *The Last Lecture* by Randy Pausch.

After my father passed away in 2006, we went through his things. He was always so full of life, and his belongings spoke of his adventures. I found photos of him as a young man playing an accordion, as a middle-aged man dressed in a Santa suit (he loved playing Santa), and as an older man, clutching a stuffed bear bigger than he was. In another photo, taken on his eightieth birthday, he was riding a roller coaster with a bunch of twenty somethings, and he had this great grin on his face.

My dad had also saved a stack of papers. There were letters regarding his insurance business and documents about his charitable projects. Then, buried in the stack, we found a citation issued in 1945, when my father was in the army. The citation for "heroic achievement" came from the commanding general of the 75th Infantry Division.

On April 11, 1945, my father's infantry company was attacked by German forces, and in the early stages of battle, heavy artillery fire led to eight casualties. According to the citation: "With complete disregard for his own safety, Private Pausch leapt from a covered position and commenced treating the wounded men while shells continued to fall in the immediate vicinity. So successfully did this soldier administer medical attention that all the wounded were evacuated successfully."

In recognition of this, my dad, then twenty-two years old, was issued the Bronze Star for valor. In the fifty years my parents were married, in the thousands of conversations my dad had with me, it had just never come up. And so there I was, weeks after his death, getting another lesson from him about the meaning of sacrifice—and about the power of humility.

I was moved to tears when I read this. In fact, the entire book is full of beautiful moments. Randy didn't have to look far for spirituality or inspiration; his father, through his own conduct, had taught him so much. Could a life be more spiritual than this? Could there be a more suitable lesson in humility than this? And why look so far, in books and stories, when I have a living, walking beacon of spirituality closer home?

Although there are countless incidents of my guru's mysticism in my everyday life, I am reminded of this incident. In 2018, Swamiji had travelled to Sydney for six weeks. In this period, he was in solitude for a fortnight, in which he finished a book on parenting titled *The Children of Tomorrow*. The rest of his time was spent in holding a meditation retreat, personal meetings with devotees and scouting for space to establish the Black Lotus Sydney Chapter.

It was the hot month of May and my sadhana was going on. Usually, in the afternoons, I would go to the temple to spend time with Sri Hari, either singing to Him or just gazing at Him lovingly.

Svadhaji would also join me sometimes, and we would laugh and joke with Sri Hari, marvelling at His beautiful, teasing smile. He understood every word and in response, His smile would grow wider, until it became an ear-to-ear grin. If you find it hard to believe how a stone idol could grin playfully, you just have to visit our temple at Sri Badrika Ashram to assuage your doubts.

One afternoon around 3 pm, Svadhaji, a talented artist and a shy person, asked me like a peevish child, 'Sadhviji, why does Swamiji go away for long periods?'

'Deep in his heart, he remains an ascetic, a detached sannyasi, *beta*,' I said to her. 'After hectic events, he likes to be in solitude,' I replied, sitting down on the steps of the *garbh-gruha*.

'But why can't he stay in the ashram and spend time with us residents, once the ashram event is over?'

'Svadhaji, as long as he is in the ashram, some issues will always need his attention. Have you not noticed how he is always sipping hot water or that ginger-tulsi concoction to soothe his throat round the year?'

She nodded, though she was not entirely convinced that she has been told the complete truth. To add weight to my argument, I explained, 'Swamiji even told us once that his throat hurts because he talks continuously, from morning to night. I really wonder how many hours he has spoken already?' I looked at Sri Hari, as if waiting for an answer.

Svadhaji soon went back to practising the harmonium and I, to my poetry writing. After the Lalita Sahasranama, at around 5.15 pm, I went to my room and checked my e-mail. There was an e-mail from Swamiji with the latest round of edits. Towards the end of the e-mail, he had written the following:

I think in the last seven years, even if we take just seven events in a year (including ashram events), and an average of four days for each event, where I would have talked for an average of six hours per day, then Sadhviji, Om Swami has already spoken for 7 years x 7 events x 4 days x 6 hours = 1176 hours!

The e-mail gave me goosebumps, and I trembled. When I told Svadhaji the exact number of hours our guru had spent speaking during ashram events in the last seven years, she wondered, 'How do you know the exact number?'

I told her about the e-mail and its timing. Her mouth fell open. A few incoherent, awe-filled words tumbled out before she could string a sentence together. 'How is that even possible? How did he hear us?'

I smiled, a superior smile as if I knew the answer to that one. 'He just does,' I said.

With a guru whose reach is beyond the stars and the Milky Way, how could I not believe in the power of a spiritual life, a grounded, virtuous life of meaning and miracles?

Many a time over the past four years, I have looked back and wondered how different my life would have been if the guidance that I have now had come my way when I was a teenager. If I knew God as I know Him now. If I had a teacher, a master, a mentor like Swamiji while I was growing up. If his teachings were known to me then, I would have shone like a diamond among pebbles, or even if I had remained a pebble, at least I would not have been rough around the edges.

This is why I feel spirituality is underrated. As adults, as children, we don't know enough about the lives of saints from different religions, our scriptures, or prayers and hymns to thank God.

Something is fundamentally wrong with our society today. There are countless temples, mosques, churches and shrines, but the people who visit them rarely inspire us. A culture of hip, fashionably spiritual people is prevalent. It is considered cool to participate in meditation camps with fancy names, remain silent for days, survive on frugal diets and so on. Does any of this really infuse any spirituality in anybody? Then there are those who completely negate God. How does one strike the right balance between modern living and spiritualism?

It is quite simple. As I see it, developing an altruistic way of thinking, living and acting is the philosophy behind all philosophies. As we cultivate talent in a child or pursue a passion, we also need to nurture and devote time to spirituality. It cannot be taken for granted any longer.

Spirituality must be cultivated as seriously as we prepare a toddler to stand on his own two feet in the world. It's what will keep him from falling when things become shaky.

For, in the absence of an inspiration, a mentor, a master and a healthy ideology to show the way ahead, we will forever remain lost and at the mercy of change in life.

The missing link

Men and women are like the two eyes in a human body—though each one sees independently, it only sees one half of life's many facets. To get the whole picture, they must both see together, side by side. Have you noticed how in our Hindu temples, *Bhagwan* in His many avatars has His consort, the Devi, by His side? Sure, there are enough stories of *Bhagwan* performing His *leela*, slaying demons, granting boons, dancing in the gardens and so on. But ultimately, even *Bhagwan* returns to His abode, a place where the Devi is once again seated by His side. The entire play of Nature rests on the play of Shiva and Shakti. What does it really mean besides the obvious?

Our greatest fulfilment comes from being at peace with the people in our lives. The love we shower upon them and the affection we receive in return makes life enjoyable. A Sunday is not really a Sunday without having a family to spend it with. A meal is merely food without children on the table to excitedly call it a feast. A life of accomplishment, accolades and achievements rings like hollow victory if life at home is a mean tug of war, a clash of the titans. The same house could be infused with love, laughter and warmth, or it could be heavy with indifference, resentment and boredom.

In films and documentaries, you often see that soldiers at the border keep a snapshot of their beloved with them. During their darkest hours, with death a bullet or a grenade away, they aren't looking at pictures of God—it is the face of a child, a wife, a girlfriend or a parent that flashes before their mind's eye. This need to love and be loved is innate.

Yet, in the name of love and togetherness, there is so much sadness everywhere. We disappoint each other at every turn. It is like a maze in which you are stuck with this other person, going through the motions of life every day with bitter resignation.

Man and woman seem to be as incompatible as an iPhone being plugged into a Samsung charging device. The vast difference in their outlooks towards life ruins any chance they might have had at happiness together. This isn't the real problem though. Differences can be sorted out; adjustments, compromises and sacrifices can be made. But inherent self-centredness cannot be changed that easily.

Each partner wants something that the other isn't willing to give—it could be their time, support, care, and sometimes, something as simple as a few soft-spoken words at the end of a gruelling day of work. There is a missing link somewhere that we can't place our finger on. Have you noticed how we hold back, waiting for the other to offer something first? Strangely, there is one thing, which if we offered to each other, we would cement our relationships and transform our lives into a sweet, playful romance.

Respect is that missing link. Respect has the softness of humility, gentleness of care and authority of love.

In the olden days, especially in Sanatana Dharma, a man possessed deep admiration for his wife, who lovingly took care of his home, ageing parents, children and him. And a wife had great respect for the man, who had vowed to take care of her in happiness and misery, all his life. I am reminded of two anecdotes that greatly put things in perspective.

Deepa, my neighbour in the city, is a woman of great faith and fortitude. In the mid-90s, as soon as she turned 16, she was married off. It was an arranged marriage. She came to live with her in-laws, their two other children and uncles and aunts. The beginning years of her marriage were a mix of growing up from a young girl to a woman and taking responsibilities that most women would shudder to think about.

At 16, she was cooking three meals for over 20 people every day and attending to other household chores, such as sweeping and mopping the huge ancestral home. She nevertheless enjoyed each moment, as there was much love and laughter in the house.

Over the next six years, however, life changed drastically for Deepa and her family, as her father-in-law's booming business suffered a sudden financial loss.

Things got so bad that their sprawling property had to be mortgaged. Creditors visited their home at odd hours and created a ruckus. With time, most creditors were paid off, except for a jeweller, who would show up every now and then asking for payment. On one such visit, Deepa saw how the jeweller's accusations brought tears to her father-in-law's eyes. He was a self-made man who had worked very hard to create his business. He was well respected in the community; a tall, proud fellow, much like her own father. She couldn't bear to see him humiliated.

On an impulse, unbeknownst to anyone, she stopped the jeweller outside the big veranda. She took off the heavy gold bangles she wore in both her hands and gave them to him. It was the last of her jewellery.

With folded hands, she said to him, 'Please take this and don't come to our house ever again. If the gold I have given you is more than the outstanding amount, and you owe me, it's no problem, you keep the rest...'

'Okay,' he said, pocketing the bangles.

'And if my father-in-law owes you more, then please let it go, because he is an old man and we have no money.'

'Hmm.' The jeweller just looked at Deepa and left the house. He never showed up again. Some weeks later, when the father-in-law bumped into the jeweller in the market and hastily tried to assure him that he would return the money soon enough, the jeweller told him, 'Your dues are cleared.'

'But how?' asked the father-in-law in utter surprise.

'Your daughter-in-law took care of it two months ago.'

Deepa was only 23 years old and already a mother of three children at the time of this incident. She mentioned it to no one except her husband and has not said a word about it to her in-laws even now. I have the greatest admiration for Deepa and have learnt many wonderful things from her.

Isn't it amazing how she acted in this situation? What would have motivated her to take this step? Was it done simply out of love, a sense of duty? Or was it the deep respect Deepa had for her in-laws and her husband that drove her to act selflessly?

Love without respect is like an overgrown garden. In the face of neglect and disrespect, it only grows weedier and wilder. All those fights in families, between couples or parents and children point to a deeper issue—a grave lack of respect.

Swamiji often says in his discourses, 'I can't make your heart gush with kindness and love for other people, but at least you can be polite and respectful under all circumstances.'

We have many false beliefs about ourselves. One of them being that not only do we deserve others' respect but we also are respectful towards them. It's not entirely true though. We may respect people's wishes, choices and outlooks in life, but we are tolerant of them only to an extent. As long as what they believe in doesn't clash with our own beliefs, it's easy to appear respectful and tolerant. Do we respect a stranger, an unknown person, or someone we've just met? It depends.

On a cloudy Saturday morning, I was putting my *dohar* outside to dry. I was in my orange night-suit (there's no escaping that colour), spreading out the soft fabric onto the wire that the neighbours had hung in the corridor to dry clothes. There are 16 flats on the sixth floor, mine being the closest to the lift.

Just then, a stocky man with a crew cut and three big tattoos running up his neck walked down the corridor. A cute boy of seven, dressed in checked knickers, white shirt, a blue tie with a school bag on his back, accompanied him. I had seen the father-son duo on several occasions; they had been my distant neighbours for the past three years. I had even exchanged a few words with his lovely wife now and then.

I had never spoken to the husband though; I had only heard him speak gruffly to his wife and child in passing. With a chewing-gum in his mouth and those menacing tattoos, he didn't seem like a very responsible person to me. That morning, as I stood there awkwardly waiting for them to pass, the big guy stopped, and without looking at me, he said to his son in a rough voice, 'Cheenu, *chalo, jai karo.*'

The child looked at me shyly, bared his little white milk teeth and bent down to touch my feet. I was taken aback by the sudden turn of events, and for a moment, I didn't know what to do.

'God bless you, *beta*,' I gently stroked Cheenu's head. Once again, without even raising his eyes to look at me (because I stood there awkwardly in my night-suit), the father gently nudged Cheenu and they were soon on their way to the school bus. I realized two things that day. One, that my neighbour was a perfectly responsible father and a gentleman, and his big tattoos and gruff voice had little to do with it. Second, that with this simple act of paying respect, he had made a place in my heart. Had I offered him the same respect at first? Had I not reserved my regard or respect based on what or who I thought was respectful? And how wrong I was!

If respecting strangers and acquaintances is important, respecting family members, friends and colleagues is paramount. It's the shortest way of keeping the heart clean, pure and free of negativity. Even if the people in your immediate circle seem rude sometimes, or seem irresponsible, neglectful and acrimonious, they don't really mean any harm. It's at best a clash of views, a passing phase that'll blow over in time.

In the end, it doesn't matter how long or mean a war we wage, when the white flag of peace is hoisted, everyone breathes a sigh of relief.

The trick with respect is that it makes it hard for us to hold grudges and behave irresponsibly or unreasonably. It's a hard stop that often halts us in our tracks as we are about to do something we might later regret. It's a technique worth trying with people you don't get along with.

In the ashram, I have an easier time now interacting with the same people I didn't get along with initially. I realized that by simply respecting their existence, talents and inherent goodness, the pointless unpleasantness could be done away with. It also gave me a window to make amends for my anti-social behaviour towards them in the past. What a lovely little thing respect is! It's like a secret spell that once cast can undo so many wrongs.

That's the thing about respect—it always compels you to act nobly. Out of deference, out of reverence, it is hard to hurt another, either with speech or action. The moment respect walks into a relationship, the relationship can never be the same again. Respect transforms love into something eternally youthful; it makes love divine.

This is a lesson I have learnt from my guru. He has a great regard for every living entity—an ant, a bird, a tree, a villager, a city dweller, rich, poor, lettered, unlettered, to him they are all the same. His words are chosen with care. His actions are packed with kindness.

Since the day I received my *sannyasa deeksha*, Swamiji has always addressed me as 'Sadhviji.' People may take my name or forget to address a sannyasi properly, but he never forgets. He always says to me, 'Only a guru is allowed to address a renunciate by her sannyasi name, but it gives me great joy to give respect to my sannyasis.' Such is the greatness of Swamiji. He, who commands our highest respect, is never disrespectful to us.

He always says, '*When you tell someone you love them, please ask yourself if you respect them, care about them. It is the only way to show how much their presence in your life truly means to you.*'

The practices that brought me here

I've discovered that God has a beautiful, kind tolerance for human flaws. He understands our ego, desires, envy and ambitions much better than we do. He is forgiving in a manner that defies belief. I have also learnt that by moulding your life in a certain way, one can get closer to Him every day. My journey towards a spiritual and meaningful life under my guru's plentiful grace has taught me many practices (call them tricks of the trade if you will). It is these practices that have led me to where I am today—still a long way from home, but a lot closer to my inner voice than I ever was.

It has taken me six long years to truly grasp the beauty and depth of Swamiji's teachings. His easy acceptance of people and his unfailing kindness has resulted in a quantum shift in my thinking. Today, I can humbly say that I am of some use to others—little, but nevertheless, some. There is great contentment in guiding lost people like myself, in helping them make their life just as joyful.

The kindness and patience with which Swamiji has put me back on my feet is perhaps the greatest gift one can bestow on a fellow human being.

It is this great wisdom—simple, practical practices— that I intend to share in the second half of this book. I call them the 'Sacred Seven.' They are sacred because they have given me:

1.   The clarity of mind and purity of heart to make sound decisions.
2.   The will to act nobly and put others' interests before my own as much as I can.

While I am no different from others and have no special achievements or accomplishments, what I do have is access to the greatest mind of all times, my guru, Om Swami. I had begun this book with a quote by Swamiji, 'Simplicity is the seed of happiness.' By simplicity, Swamiji means that we should learn to enjoy life. The myriad activities that add colour, fun and playfulness to our day need to be savoured.

In this mad race of earning, commuting, putting food in our overstuffed tummies or doing things for our loved ones, we are too preoccupied with the nitty-gritty of living. It is all happening to us, like pre-programmed commands in a piece of software. There is no room to evolve, learn or play something new. That newness is absent. The joy of pursuing a long-cherished childhood dream or taking out time for a long-lost passion is pushed to the back of a drawer like a pair of old socks.

You might say that an average life consists of a lot of work and a bit of fun, love and celebration. But just living a life doesn't necessarily mean you are savouring and appreciating it. These are the motions of existence that one goes through anyway. Is there anything that gets you out of bed every day with the thought, 'Today, I can do so much more?' How many people can truly say that about their lives?

The monotony and melancholy of everyday living stops us from seeing the beauty in our surroundings, in other people and in ourselves. If we could learn to go easy and work towards self-improvement and self-purification with zeal and enthusiasm, we will find new learnings knocking on our door every day. Life is, after all, about learning, making mistakes and relearning.

It's true that we forget these learnings faster than a child moves on from one toy to another, but it's also true that some of it invariably stays with us, changing us in big and small measures.

It is with this faith and surrender at Swamiji's divine feet that I lay before you what I have indeed learnt from him and has worked for me through these seven unfailing practices.

Sadhvi Vrinda handing a copy of *The Book of Faith*,
compiled by her, to Swamiji.

Book II
The Sacred Seven

In goodness
the inner world is built
brick by brick
beam by beam
As the subtle breeze
of silence blows
and gentle clouds
of quietude
roam the sky
there sprouts in
the hearts of men
a divine seed
of pure and
unbounded joy

A prayer that never fails

Years ago, I wrote the following poem:

Life without love
Is like a park without children
Bereft of laughter, of innocence
Like a temple without God
A book without a reader
A man without a woman

There is a general misconception that a renunciate has no place for love in her life. After all, she has embraced the ochre to drown herself in detachment and dispassion. Strangely, the more you walk on the spiritual path, the more you realize how love is the very basis of all creation. I don't know about others, but I just had to have more love. Sure, I had been disappointed in love and had done my share of disappointing as well; yet, the heart, for as long as it beats, is filled with a yearning to care and be cared for. Never will you find a parent whose heart no longer beats for her child.

Love is inevitable, just like life and death. It was only a matter of time before I fell in love; my guru and his cause were more love-worthy than I had ever envisioned anything or anyone to be. It was the most natural thing to find, this love growing in my heart. However, it wasn't enough. My quest was not over, my thirst was alive. I was in search of a love in which there would be no room for disappointments, no place for impermanence.

Swamiji often says, *'Don't just fall in love, rise in it. Love more than just a person; fall in love with a cause, an activity, an ideology, something bigger and far greater than yourself.'*

It wasn't easy finding something so priceless. A year passed by with no change; and then another year and another. Three years passed by, and I felt little more than affection and adoration for that beautiful, black stone idol that we addressed as Sri Hari in the temple. It all began to change in 2017.

After a three-month sadhana in the ashram, I finally fell in love with Lord Narayana, one of the many holy names of Sri Hari. No longer did the beautiful feet of the *vigraha* appear like they were carved of black stone; instead, the dark colour of rain clouds seemed to adorn His feet. Lord Narayana, known for His dark blue colouring—*meghavarnam* (the colour of clouds)—had assumed the shape of a person for me. His playful smile and teasing ways, the manner in which He fulfilled wishes quietly, I saw them all. I fought with Him. I loved Him dearly. I took from Him as a child takes from a parent. I made demands on His time, as one makes demands on the time of a beloved. In *Bhagwan*, I had found the perfect companion.

My inner life and spiritual quest took on a new meaning. The flaws were still there, but love had mellowed them. I saw my mistakes more clearly. He helped me see and hear things that I had not been prepared to admit or listen to earlier. In love, I was willing to change. The desire to purify myself for Him had taken on a new life. My perspective underwent a sea change, and I wanted to be of service to others.

It was as if a new person was emerging from beneath the older one. **Divine Love was my undoing**. It moulded me bit by bit to follow my dharma.

Bhagwan became the great presence in my life who drove me to try and live in grace and harmony with myself and others. He alone giveth, is what I truly came to understand.

We all need this purity, this divinity in our lives, because everything falls apart in its absence. Our search for meaning, purpose and a fulfilling life is all but a ruse to find God.

It is this prayer to be worthy of God that never fails. A prayer for constant self-improvement and self-purification. It is the only prayer that never fails.

Find Him in any shape or form, in any religion or scripture, but find Him. You are incomplete without Him, for in love alone, one is complete.

It is this prayer that God has answered for me. In His answers, I found a beautiful pattern that demanded hard work, discipline and a truthful life. I had to make a humongous effort to train my mind to lead a meaningful life.

For is it not the mind that binds us to our fearful past, remorseful present and ambiguous future? The mind's ability to create our own personal hell needs no introduction. In time, I understood that control of the mind brings liberation. And this liberation can only be achieved by a deliberate, conscious effort to weed the mind of negativity. This practice alone is the basis of all spiritual practices. It is the purification of the mind that leads to better control of our thoughts, feelings and emotions.

There is no hell if the mind stays unruffled in the face of a crisis. There is no crisis, if in the midst of a situation, the mind remains perfectly calm and functional. A calm mind is the hallmark of an evolved person.

Swamiji has always maintained that the best way to gauge your spiritual progress is to see how easily and how many times a day you get disturbed. Our minds, like overburdened servers, are forever down. When you constantly monitor your thoughts and feelings, all the stored up negativity starts to thaw. As the slow meltdown begins, you start to see your blind spots clearly, and correcting them then becomes child's play. A new way of thinking starts to take shape, and the seed of mindfulness is sown.

Just as a mother watches her baby grow into a wise young adult, you watch yourself blossom into a person of great calm and reserve. The clarity of mind that comes in the wake of this new consciousness is the fruit of all the practices. It is the ultimate prize. How did I go about earning this prize? Well, I was crawling on all fours, but I got there alright.

O Bhagwan,
I pray from the shallow depths of my being
that I cast this world aside
for the sweet prize of your name

Immersed in your glory
I neither know time nor days
I have no friend no foe
in harmony I sing

There be no envy in my heart
no claims to stake
the symphony of your love alone
keep out the worldly play

Oh, dear Narayana
Your abode alone I see
A place one day where I'll rest
my head upon your knee

Oh, let me forget this world
and be in yours while I still live
Your worship be my breath
Your name the elixir I drink

I have no patience for me
this silliness will never end
Like a child holding on to a parent
I cling to your divine feet

I remember nothing and no one
except the beauty of your form
only your words reach my ears
and all noises scatter and fall

Oh, Bhagwan, always know my heart
You alone purify me
You alone keep me safe
Your love alone is transcendental bliss

I pray.

I now present to you these seven sacred practices whose simplicity belies the great power that resides in them.

*Punarapi jananaṃ punarapi maraṇaṃ,punarapi
janani jaṭhare śayanam |
iha saṃsāre bahudustāre,kṛpayā'pāre pāhi murāre.*

Once again that birth, that death and going back in
the womb. This is a difficult world; please help me
out of this, O Lord.

—Adi Shankaracharya

1
Be inspired

An inspiration, an ideology, a role model, give it any name you like, was always missing from my life. I did not have anyone who could inspire me to lead a meaningful life, nor did I feel any pressing need to change my way of life. You see, all these theories about a life of meaning and purpose sound like bull until life hits you on the head. It is only when things start going from bad to worse that you realize that you need to do something about it. That quest invariably brings you to something or someone that motivates you to abandon your old way of thinking.

Through the big crises in my life, I had no motivation to change. Where was I going? What did I really want out of life? I had no answers. It is not that at 32 years of age, I was too old to be inspired; I was just too jaded to find inspiration anymore. Even if I wanted to turn my life around, I had no idea about whom I could aspire to be. Whom could I turn to when I didn't even know what I was looking for?

Years after meeting my guru, I realized that having a role model early on in life is like having a small stock of savings that you can draw upon in hard times. It keeps you up and running until you can chalk out a concrete plan. People who have inspiration—whether in the form of living or dead gurus, great leaders, books, quotes, melodies or individuals—are more likely to find their way out of a crisis.

I remember the first time when I felt inspired to change my way of life. Like an expecting mother feels the first movement of the foetus in her womb, I felt the first stirring of the want to lead a simple life while reading the manuscript of Swamiji's memoir, *If Truth Be Told*, in 2013.

I thought, here was someone my age, who had not only accomplished so much, but had also given it all up for a singular goal. It was thought-provoking on a deeply personal level. I wondered whether educated men really went chasing God in the Himalayas. If they did, I had never heard of them.

The hardships Swamiji had weathered in that extreme climate and the sheer bliss that he was immersed in day and night was like reading about a time out of mind. His drive to gain the divine vision and lead a life of truth and simplicity appealed to someone like me, whose life was more complicated than a TV drama.

Before him, I had never been inspired to live a life other than what I knew. It was like wanting to clean up after a terrible hangover. I wanted to be presentable and join my family the next morning at the breakfast table with my chin up and head held high. I was ready for a simple life. I had begun to realize that a life of truth and goodness was possible in this day and age. I had someone to look up to, in whose footsteps I could not only walk but I could also carve my own path, for he encouraged everyone to discover their own truth.

Eventually, I figured that if reading about this person's life could spark such a change in my perspective, what would he be like in person? The rest, as they say, is history. I went to meet Swamiji in his ashram and was bowled over by his spirit of service and compassion. I wanted to be like him.

I remember this incident from 2014, in the first couple of months at the ashram, when there were only five residents. I possessed a stubbornness, an arrogance that landed me in trouble sometimes. With a certain construction worker from the village, I just couldn't hold my tongue. The argument soon turned into a big row over how I had insulted a 16-year-old juvenile. Of course, none of the villagers present were willing to admit that I was compelled to defend myself when the young boy had started spouting swear words at me. But my guru trusted me over all the people and their petty complaints.

I thanked him profusely for backing me. I asked, 'Swamiji, why do you tolerate me? Why do you not turn me away?'

Raising his eyes to the false ceiling, he replied, 'Think about it. What if Buddha had walked away from Angulimala? There would have been no great transformation...'

'Am I Angulimala?' I exclaimed.

Swamiji laughed softly and said, 'Before Valmiki wrote the great epic, *Ramayana*, he was a notorious dacoit. Had the eternal itinerant Narada not helped him realize the truth, he would never have become the great sage he went on to be.' He paused and then added, 'My job is to show you the right conduct, the highest ideal, so that it inspires you to live up to your full potential—the real you.'

* * *

Over the next six years, Swamiji inspired me every day to better myself, to be gentle, sensitive and kind to others. It is his inspiration alone that has changed the course of my life.

If you think you don't need inspiration or a mentor in life, you are in for a rude shock. The moment your ship hits the tidal waves of great challenges and unmanageable struggles, you will find yourself stripped of your strengths of reserve and composure. It feels as if all the windowpanes of your home have been shattered by a big explosion. Your house is still standing, but it is little more than a shell, a heap of rubble and wreckage. It is as if you are standing on the pavement, and all the debris from your crumbling life is raining upon your head.

Today, we don't even have to picture such terrifying scenarios as sudden illnesses or accidents; something as simple as a few professional failures can turn the most happy-go-lucky person into a withering mess. A normal family life is enough to drive you into clinical depression.

Like a clueless meteor in space, you find yourself travelling through unknown galaxies of emotions and feelings. Mental health today is one of the most neglected aspects of our culture, and without any hope or help, it is difficult to navigate these vast unknowns.

This is where inspiration saunters in like a cool maiden enjoying the evening breeze. What a refreshing sight it is to see her carefree spirit, the wind softly blowing her hair away from her face, gently ruffling the hem of her dress! Not a care in the world, not a frown to mar her serene face. What would an injured spirit not give to be in her invigorating presence? Give your inspiration a face, a name; identify with it. Today, to have inspiration—living or dead, animate or inanimate, someone to spark the fire of change, simplicity and truth in you—is like having a pill of self-confidence and clarity with you at all times.

During a crisis, all you have to do is pop some inspiration into yourself, and you are back on your feet to troubleshoot and firefight. There is no confusion then, you simply have to think what your role model would have done in the circumstances, how he would have acted. Then the path ahead becomes clear.

It is what really brings me back whenever I digress from my path—knowing how my master would act, speak or be. It is difficult to then make mistakes, and when I do make them, I also know how he would make up for them. And I am quick to make amends.

There is no confusion when you have an inspiration in your life. The principles and values of the person who inspires you become yours, and you feel more grounded and decisive than you have ever felt in your life. It is not long before you too become someone's inspiration.

Stay forever inspired.

2
Admit that you are less than perfect

Think about the one person in the world whom you love the most. The image of your child, partner or parent might rush to your mind. But that would be only half the truth. The one you love the most is, really, yourself. This self-love is so good at hiding itself that most people lead their entire lives not knowing how much they love themselves.

As a child, I loved watching cartoons. When Jerry, the mouse, led Tom, the cat, on a chase around the house, I always thought how lucky they were to get to play the whole day. While I had to go to school and cram new things into my little head, Spiderman was swinging from building to building, having fun and busting robbers. I wanted to be a part of their exciting world. Their life seemed so carefree. I could be one of them too, I would think. It never occurred to me that these extraordinary characters existed only on screen, that they weren't real.

Just as a child takes the make-believe world to be real, we grown-ups too weave our universe around ourselves. In this universe, we are our own superheroes. We can't do anything wrong. Any mistakes that we make, any flaws that we might possess, are little more than quirks or oddities, and endearing ones at that. It's so difficult to see oneself in a harsh light. We are our own biggest fans. We couldn't possibly be misguided or dishonest, quarrelsome or egoistic. These adjectives apply to others;

we are exempted from them by simply being who we are, our own ardent lovers.

It never occurs to us that if others are rude or discourteous to us, it may be because of our behaviour towards them. I am not talking about the law of attraction here, but simply acting with courtesy and humility towards a fellow human being. You may wonder, 'Since when has being nice and polite been the solution to life's big problems?' True, it isn't. But it does make life easier when you are looked upon as someone who is friendly and bankable.

Isn't it true that we lose our patience, kindness, care and temper more often than we care to admit? We repeatedly make the same mistakes without ever admitting to having made them. The cause of our sorrows, in our eyes, always seems to lie elsewhere. We rarely point a finger at ourselves. There is always someone or something handy to blame for all that is not right in life.

These blind spots that we all possess are the biggest hurdles on the path of self-improvement. We must learn to see our own faults.

Examine your conduct, and check if it is your ego hiding behind the mask of politeness or pretence behind an act of goodness. Any falsity in our conduct only breeds more suffering. For instance, in an argument, when both people are screaming at the top of their lungs to be heard, who's to say who's right? Any valid point that one may have had is already lost in the noise and race of being right and indignant.

It never occurs to us that we need to take responsibility for the way our life has turned out. The only questions Swamiji ever asks me when I make a mistake are, 'What is your fault in the given situation? Could you have acted differently?'

In the ground-breaking book, *The Road Less Travelled* by M. Scott Peck, there is a great anecdote about how people avoid taking a hard look at themselves.

> We cannot solve life's problems except by solving them. This statement may seem idiotically tautological or self-evident, yet it is seemingly beyond the comprehension of much of the human race.
>
> The extent to which people will go psychologically to avoid assuming responsibility for personal problems, while always sad, is sometimes almost ludicrous.
>
> A career sergeant in the army, stationed in Okinawa and in serious trouble because of his excessive drinking, was referred for psychiatric evaluation and, if possible, assistance.
>
> He denied that he was an alcoholic, or even that his use of alcohol was a personal problem, saying, "There's nothing else to do in the evenings in Okinawa except drink."
>
> "Do you like to read?" I asked.
>
> "Oh yes, I like to read, sure."
>
> "Then why don't you read in the evening instead of drinking?"
>
> "It's too noisy to read in the barracks."
>
> "Well, then, why don't you go to the library?"
>
> "The library is too far away."
>
> "Is the library farther away than the bar you go to?"
>
> "Well, I'm not much of a reader. That's not where my interests lie."
>
> "Do you like to fish?" I then inquired.

> "Sure, I love to fish."
>
> "Why not go fishing instead of drinking?"
>
> "Because I have to work all day long."
>
> "Can't you go fishing at night?"
>
> "No, there isn't any night fishing in Okinawa."
>
> "But there is," I said. "I know several organizations that fish at night here. Would you like me to put you in touch with them?"
>
> "Well, I really don't like to fish."
>
> "What I hear you saying," I clarified, "is that there are other things to do in Okinawa except drink, but the thing you like to do most in Okinawa is drink."
>
> "Yeah, I guess so."
>
> "But your drinking is getting you in trouble, so you're faced with a real problem, aren't you?"
>
> "This damn island would drive anyone to drink."
>
> I kept trying for a while, but the sergeant was not the least bit interested in seeing his drinking as a personal problem which he could solve either with or without help, and I regretfully told his commander that he was not amenable to assistance. His drinking continued, and he was separated from the service in mid-career.

This is how most of us live, in a fool's paradise, thinking that others are the source of our grievances, that these problems are anything but self-created. These blind spots—this complete oblivion to our own flaws—make us hold the world, the people in it, our well-wishers, responsible for the big and small disturbances in our life. Even the most intelligent and balanced people run away from assuming responsibility for the problems in their lives. It could be false pride, ignorance or plain blindness that makes us ignore our own faults. Swamiji would often smilingly tell me that I lived in my own little bubble. I presumed at that time that he meant it as a good thing.

The truth is that for a problem to be addressed, we must first peep into our hearts to see whether *we* are the cause of it, whether a dominant trait in us causes these daily behavioural malfunctions. Once you start recognizing your blind spots, correcting them becomes easier. An exercise that really comes in handy in course-correction is visualization. Visualization helps to frequently clean up all the muck that keeps gathering in our hearts. I call this process **The Clean-Up.**

THE CLEAN-UP

Fundamental. Inevitable.

If you are a gentle, soft-spoken, mild-mannered person, who generally remains calm and dignified as you walk through the high gates of joy and the lone alleys of darkness, well, then you can skip this section right away, hop over it, as a child jumps over a dirty puddle. You are clearly a demi-god. If, however, you are arrogant, conceited, prone to bouts of anger, envy and intolerable thinking, and lack the humility to treat some people with respect, then, welcome to the club.

You might think that these are harsh words to describe myself (or you), but the truth is worse than this. We aren't very pleasant to look at in the harsh light of truth. Our true identities lie beneath our social images. The real thoughts behind our polite chats and our generous actions aren't always altruistic or kind, they are quite twisted sometimes. The man or woman behind the mask is quite different from the one who walks around in the world, being amiable, pleasing and attractive to behold. It must feel like I'm trying to make us out to be perpetrators of some great crime. Leading an unhappy, unfulfilling life is not a crime. Neither is it a crime to allow that unhappiness to run and ruin the lives of those connected to us. It's a way of life; live, don't live, but definitely not let others live in peace.

In his book, *A Million Thoughts,* Swamiji has penned this beautiful passage on why man remains unhappy through the course of his life. How his thoughts, speech and actions are never in harmony. And anything that is not in harmony in the play of nature is forced to align. Suffering, Swamiji says, is alignment.

'And to the one whose thoughts, speech and actions are in harmony, to such a person, suffering has no more impact than a cloth of silk rubbing against an elephant.'

What a profound statement!

We are indeed creating our own personal hell. The next question is, then, how do we experience inner calm? My mind, which I compare to a house here, has always been in disarray—thoughts, speech and action, all possessing a mind of their own, having their separate, independent rooms, like quarrelsome siblings who never really get along. The more I thought about it, it occurred to me that we would have to first clean the space from where all the thoughts, actions and speech originate: our minds. We have to clean up our mental space as diligently as one cleans a dirty room, inch by inch.

Sometimes, when I get buried too deep under the weight of my mistakes, I do these visualizations. And keep up the momentum spanning a few days, weeks, many times a day, until my mind feels cleaner, emptier and free of all the trash. The power of visualization is tremendous; it's like creating a parallel universe where you run your own show, where you are the protagonist, the author of your own story, as well as the director, cast and crew.

In a nutshell, visualization is reinventing yourself. It's a balm to the wounded, a mighty herb that keeps you warm in the cold, desolate winter of hopelessness. Try it, if you don't believe me.

1. The Broomstick Visualization

In the morning when you wake up, keep lying in bed a little longer. Imagine holding a long broomstick in your hand, as you move about in an open field, clearing fallen leaves and pebbles from the ground. You are walking with the broom in your hand, gently but firmly clearing your path. The more you clean, more the ground underneath starts to take shape. With each stroke of the broom, dust is rising in the air, fading away, giving way to clean ground beneath your feet. This field is the space in your head.

Look far and wide at the beautiful view this uncluttered space has allowed you. In whichever direction you look, there's only air and more fresh air to breathe. Nothing is obstructing your view. Your mind is getting cleaner, emptier—just as you would like it to be. Enjoy this refreshing change from how crowded with thoughts and to-do-lists your mind usually is. This open space in your mind is rejuvenating, for you hold nothing against anyone, not even yourself. All you experience are open spaces above and clean ground beneath your feet. This is how your mind now looks.

Empty. Free. Open.

During the day, if any thought, emotion, conversation or event disturbs you, quickly grab your broomstick and start sweeping your mental space, clearing it of the negative emotions that have suddenly risen on the horizon to steal your peace.

This peace of mind is the only piece of your mindspace that's worth a fortune on the spiritual landscape. When someone's telling me something that I either don't wish to hear or have no choice but to listen to, I now start to sweep my mental space to clear this new influx of unwanted information. Using an imaginary broom has suddenly become a great new hobby.

2. The Mansarovar Visualization

What if one day I could see the true me, the purity that resides in me? What would she look like? I don't know. But what if I could perceive her? If I could see who I could be, it would be like having a glimpse of a future that has remained elusive all of my adult life. What if I could bring that illusion to life? Breathe life into it and see the other me?

It so happened, and I don't know when, except after a moment of great insanity, I found myself near a pristine lake, still and silent, the Kailash Mansarovar. It was as if a mammoth piece of glass had been laid horizontally onto the ground, shimmering, crystal-like, filling me with piety. As I peeped into the looking glass, I saw my reflection looking back at me—a serene face with clear eyes, guileless, staring at me and smiling. She, the other me, was white like the snow that surrounded the blue water. Not a frown to mar her innocence. Youthful like a child-goddess, she seemed free. In that sacred land of Kailash, the lake of the gentle *hamsas*, I sat by the still waters, experiencing my immaculate self—a self that is devoid of flaws, someone who is tranquil and generous. She is me, I thought.

I didn't know if I would ever really be her. But the possibility existed. And so I tried to embrace her with all my might. 'One day, I'm going to catch you,' I said to the reflection in the water.

I stayed there for a little while, and then it slipped away into the depths of my consciousness, from where it had sprung in the first place. It had no basis in my physical reality, you may say. But think again. An unalloyed, flawless you must exist. If it didn't, what is the whole strife about finding your true self, anyway?

These visualizations are mere examples. You could create your own visualization techniques—anything that resonates with you, inspires you and strengthens you. Your own little movie of who you could be. It's a beautiful hope to hand yourself when the inner world is dark and in need of a ray of light.

The second sacred step towards self-purification is to admit the problem areas in your life and find a way to clean up your act.

Admit your flaws, clean yourself up.

3
Wonder

In the Oxford Dictionary, the word 'wonder' is assigned the following meaning:

A feeling of surprise and admiration that you have when you see or experience something beautiful, unusual or unexpected.

We know what it feels to feel wonder and awe. It may not happen often, but every once in a while, life elicits an innocent, awe-filled smile from us. Our eyes shine with laughter, our faces glow with amazement and our bodies beam with pleasure at something unexpectedly touching or heart-warming.

Try to recollect the last time you looked up at the sky and thought what a wonder it was to live under an azure blue sky. When was the last time you looked with awe at the faces of the little idols stacked in your altar and thought how real they appeared? Or looked with wonder at the lingering happiness on someone's face? Most of you will be able to think of an incident or two; life has a way of enticing wonder even in the most unyielding, grumpy mind. Wonder is a scarce commodity. It exists, but it doesn't. It's there, and it isn't. (Cryptic!)

Our experience of the world within and without is so shrouded in busyness—mental, physical and emotional—that we rarely ever display that childlike admiration for life that we used to have. Fraught, saddened and anxious, we look for happiness, reassurance and faith everywhere but in ourselves. Will we find outside what we carry within us? A devotee once asked Ramana Maharishi if it would be possible to prostrate before him and touch his feet. He made the following response:

'*The real feet of* Bhagwan *exist only in the heart of the devotee. To hold on to these feet incessantly is true happiness. You will be disappointed if you hold on to my physical feet, because one day this physical body will disappear. The greatest worship is worshipping the guru's feet that are within oneself.*'

What do we find when we look within ourselves? Do we see *Bhagwan's* feet; do we see our guru seated there? It's a good question to pose to ourselves: Is our belief held in place by tender strings of outwardly reverence or a deep connect with our object of faith?

As a sannyasi, I worshipped my guru and our deity and felt great awe and admiration in my heart. Yet, at the first sign of failure or sorrow in any aspect of my life, my belief would start to disintegrate like a wet paper boat. The new ochre robe, responsibilities and a new name and title could uplift me mentally and socially, but spiritual uplifting needed a great leap of faith.

In November 2017, we had the first Gayatri Sadhana camp in the ashram. During the three-day camp, after Swamiji's discourse, I would lead the morning session of chanting the Gayatri Mantra, while the afternoon session was led by Swami Paramananda. It was indeed an auspicious feeling to hear the sound of the sacred mantra reverberating in the temple in sweet symphony with the birds chirping outside.

It is quite cold in the ashram in November, and I was layered in woollens. I remember taking off a black glove to hold the rudraksha beads before the chanting. My hands felt icy.

I sat on a little raised platform, facing 200 people immersed in chanting the mantra, and a beautiful, infallible energy permeated the temple. I wondered what these people would say if they knew that I had initially found the Gayatri Mantra a bit too long for my taste and had opted to do a different sadhana.

I loved Mother Divine in my own childish, playful ways, and had often crawled into Her lap in my many visualizations in the past. To me, mantra *japa* was fun, only because I could be a child again and play with the Universal Mother, reliving my lost childhood.

I had done a long Devi sadhana earlier that year but had shied away from the Gayatri Mantra sadhana, as I found the mantra long-winded (I've always been a lazy sannyasi).

Before leading the chanting session, I paid obeisance to my guru and sought his blessings. I then chanted the mantra out loud for the first seven counts and then fell silent doing my *manasik* (mental) *japa*, while many people chose to chant the mantra out loud. For the next 30 minutes, the sound of the sacred mantra poured in like a gushing river. The first day of the morning session had passed quite pleasantly. It was as if bliss had invaded the cold and was now seeping into our hearts and minds. I felt Ma's presence most acutely. She had to come; Mother Divine always arrives with just one call from Swamiji.

On the second day of the camp, once again, I felt great waves of love, or call it energy if you will, flowing from the *vigraha* of Sri Hari. Ved Mata Gayatri, tall and fulsome, clad in a white sari, the pleats falling at her feet like garlands of fragrant flowers, stood behind my asana, radiating energy in the dark. Aware of the big, warm, gentle whiteness behind me, I felt great bliss in my heart. It was a most unusual visualization, because I hadn't imagined it. It had come to my mind of its own accord. I wasn't the maker of this vision that had unfurled like a flower; it had sprung up most unexpectedly.

The awareness of Her gentle presence was so powerful that I opened my eyes at the same moment that the chanting got over. A hush had fallen over the temple, as people savoured their experiences in their minds. Smiling like an overfed Buddha, I looked all around at the happy, drawn, crying and peaceful faces. My rational mind dismissed my experience as a figment of my imagination and considered it an absolute no-no to make tall public statements such as, 'Behold people, Ved Mata Gayatri is here,' as if I was some great *tapasvi* who had summoned the goddess with my immaculate *japa.* So, while my mind scoffed at the temerity of my consciousness, my mouth blurted out these tall claims anyway.

'Ma is here,' I said. 'I feel as if She stands behind me. She is clad in a silvery-white sari, beautiful and radiant. Love and grace flow from Her, feel Her presence...'

I said a few more things of which I have no recollection. I just remember feeling this great fervour, wanting people to experience the same warmth that I felt behind me. With my guru's *tapas* alone, it was made possible that Mother Divine dwelled in our quaint temple in the *vigraha*. And now that She had stepped out, I wished everyone could feel what I was feeling. A part of my mind chided me, wanting me to stop sounding so righteous and preachy, but I didn't really care what people thought. She was here. Seeing those 200 faces looking at me, some with awe and belief, others with disbelief or wonder, I couldn't help asking, 'Did anyone else experience what I did?'

And there in the second row to my left, a hand went up.

'You did?' I was now looking at a man of sombre bearing. Kailas nodded, and I could barely contain my excitement. You cannot imagine how thrilled I was. What a relief it was to know that I wasn't alone, that my juvenile mind hadn't just made it all up.

'Oh, this person looks like a serious *sadhaka*!' I thought to myself.

Surely, Ma revealed herself to him. And that was indeed the best part, for this person seemed like a steadfast *sadhaka* and not a muddled, self-doubting, newbie sannyasi like me. I was greatly reassured that if another person had sensed what I had (one who even had the air of a serious bhakta), then my experience was very real. In that moment, I felt greatly encouraged and felt my faith strengthen.

However, this is only half the story. When I first thought of including this anecdote in the book, I decided to write to Kailas, who lives in the US, to share his version of the event. Here it is, two sides of the same story. What a beautiful thing perspective is!

In Kailas's words:

My Experience at the first Gayatri Sadhana Camp 2017

I had taken to Gayatri Sadhana, predominantly during the four *navratras* (nine holy days of Mother Divine) and as part of my *nitya karma* (daily practice), ever since I met *param pujya* Swamiji in 2013. He had advised me to tread the path. I hadn't been consistent initially and struggled for a while. I was never a religious person and could hardly sit still for a few minutes at a time.

Over a period of time, I had reached out to Swamiji for guidance and course correction of my practice. So, when the first camp was announced, I jumped at the opportunity and booked my spot. I arrived at the ashram for the first time on the eve of November 23, 2017, in time for the evening *arti*. Basking in the bliss and soaking it all in, I was at peace. The next morning, my roommate and I went out for a walk down to the river Giri-Ganga. On our way back, at the top, up where the road from ashram begins towards the river, stood a radiant *yogin* in ochre, and my first instinct was to bow down at her feet.

She immediately said, 'There is some quiet energy about you that I like. Whatever the purpose you have come for, it will be accomplished on this—your first—visit to the ashram.'

I was taken aback as to how she knew this was my first visit. I did not question her and walked away. Not knowing who she was added to the mystery.

The next day, during the discourse, *param pujya* Swamiji introduced her to the audience and said that Sadhviji would lead us in the chanting and meditation practice of the Gayatri Mantra during the morning sessions. Though I had read her book, *Om Swami – As We Know Him*, from her *poorva-ashram* (before renunciation) days, this was my first introduction to Sadhviji. I said to myself, 'This was who I met this morning, what grace!'

The next morning, after Swamiji's discourse, I happened to be in the second or third row from the front and the second person from the aisle. Sadhviji sat just outside the chrome railings, a few feet away from me, to lead the meditation. Once we settled down, she began the session by invoking the Divine Mother in the form of Ma Gayatri. It was an incredible experience for me as she invoked Ma, as I could 'perceive' Ma walking out of Sri Hari and standing behind Sadhviji. For my rational mind, it was unacceptable. It had never happened to me before. I opened my eyes to see if it was 'really' so.

No, my physical eyes did not see it. Again, when I got back into meditation, I could perceive the wave of energy and Ma's presence, standing right behind Sadhviji. I held on until the end of the session and shared my excitement with my roommate immediately thereafter. I asked him if he had felt so too. His answer was in the negative. Well, my mind could be playing games, I thought.

The following morning, Sadhviji led the session again. This time, I requested my roommate for the aisle seat, and I got it. Sadhviji was right in front of me. She invoked Ma Gayatri in the form of Ma Saraswati, and again, Ma walked out of Sri Hari and stood behind Sadhviji. I did not open my eyes, I held on—for the session—for an incredible experience. I did not want the session to end, and it seemed like it had lasted for only a few minutes.

My mind now needed validation. Did this really happen? Sadhviji invokes Ma, and She, ever so lovingly comes down to be by her side? It was then that Sadhviji asked the audience whether anyone else had felt Ma standing behind her. I raised my hand. I had so many questions I wanted to ask her. After the session, I walked up to Sadhviji and told her what I had felt with my mind's eye. She gave me a smile that is etched in my memory.

It has been a year since I completed Ma Gayatri's *anushthan*, by the grace of *param pujya* Swamiji. I now realize that some experiences are not to be looked at from a rational mind or questioned. They just have to be accepted as they are.

—Kailas

I hope you understand why I wanted you to know Kailas's version. Both of us had sought external validation for the beautiful phenomenon that we had undoubtedly experienced. While I had thought, 'Here's a great Devi bhakta. If he also saw what I saw, then my experience must be real.' On Kailas's part, he knew little of my own mental confusion and regarded me as an adept and was thrilled to have his vision validated by my own experience.

The point that I wish to make is that there is wonder and awe in plenty in our lives. Beautiful things—surreal, unearthly or divine—happen to all of us, irrespective of whether we are great believers in a particular god or philosophy. But we are ready to believe in everyone but ourselves. We have so little faith in the purity of our own being, of what our minds are capable of perceiving and conceiving that the wonders of existence, of our own beautiful self are wasted on us.

On the path of self-purification, your ability to feel awed and amazed by little things every day will keep your spiritual zest alive. Belief in your believing will infuse your life with magic.

There's a beautiful song by ABBA that sums up 'wonder' in these lines:

If you see the wonder of a fairy tale,

You can take the future even if you fail...

Never let the lamp of wonder and awe be snuffed out from your heart. Carry, every single day, an unwavering anticipation of wonderful things to unfold. In our darkest, bleakest moments, let us know that there is great beauty in this life waiting to be discovered and explored. Unspoilt treasures lie within. Our higher self is as real and tangible as our breath. We need to slowly learn to trust our own instincts, our own magical inner voice.

Live a life of *wonder* every day.

4
Self-discipline:
The big secret

The way to bring order to even the most directionless life is to lead a life grounded in discipline. Discipline has a way of curbing even the most rampant chaos in the head. It is the big secret behind the *tapas* of the sages of yore that helped them accomplish amazing feats. It is the discipline of mind and body that led my guru to discover his own truth, while he sat unmoving for 22 hours, every day for seven months, in single-minded concentration. His ultimate goal—a union with the Divine.

Today, when devotees come to seek Swamiji's darshan after having read his books, they are smitten by his radiance. The gentle ripples of love and warmth that emanate from him are a constant source of wonder and curiosity. The iron will behind his delicate exterior exudes a divine luminosity that even a non-believer finds hard to resist. You ask him the secret behind this divine glow and he answers jokingly, 'A good moisturizer!'

Well, that's one hell of a moisturizer that can keep you rooted in humility and compassion. The truth is that discipline is like a gentle massaging of the soul, a spiritual equivalent of getting the blood circulation going.

By discipline here, I'm not referring to waking, sleeping, eating and working at the same time every day, for most people do stick to some kind of routine in their lives. Then how is having a routine different from having discipline? The difference is in the outcome. You could perform the same activity every single day and not gain much from it. It could leave you unfulfilled and just as jaded as when you started. Discipline, on the other hand, is a self-rewarding exploit; the act of pursuing the discipline itself is your reward.

In most Hindu homes, you have an altar where a lamp is lit morning and evening; it is a practice that has been followed generation after generation. However, whether it makes people any more spiritual or compassionate is debatable. The lamp surely burns bright in their homes, but do their hearts experience calmness and peace? Not necessarily. On the other hand, a person may sit down to meditate or chant a hymn in front of the altar to experience something new. And that day will come indisputably when the purity of his sentiment will start to reflect in his conduct and appearance. The strength of his discipline will bring about a subtle change at first, and with time, a more noticeable, comprehensive change. He will start to become his discipline.

The sheer power of performing a productive activity with single-minded focus every day cannot be emphasized enough. It becomes a prayer. I first heard this analogy from Swamiji when he sat down to play Chopin's Nocturne in C sharp minor.

'Do you know why great music maestros compare their practice and their art to a divine union with God?' Swami Vidyananda and I exchanged a dumb look and shook our heads in unison.

'They have become their music. Some call it *riyaz* (daily practice); others call it worship.'

This act of daily worship, when applied to any area in your life, is bound to bring an extraordinary stillness of the mind, where you are lost in the world of your own creation, passion or hobby. In the beginning, the world of your creation, the time and space you've carved out for yourself, will waver like a bad TV signal; you will have clarity of mind and thought in patches. But as your practice grows, so will your inner calm and peace. Yes, it might not be as long-lasting as you would like it to be. But to live in a state of clarity, even for a short while, is a rare blessing.

The act of pursuing a fulfilling and meaningful activity, and seeing it through every single day, brings about a great transformation in the psyche of even the most wandering minds.

When people approach me in the ashram, their hearts heavy with sorrow, grief, disenchantment and the monotony of life and its blows and shakedowns, I don't have any great advice to dispense. It simply comes down to asking, 'What are you committed to in life?' My guru's whole life is committed to being compassionate and truthful. His most practical advice has always been to the point.

'It is by practice alone that you can override the tendencies of the mind.'

It is his practical approach to life and its problems that has always appealed to and worked for me. Some people come to him looking for mystical answers and miraculous cures to their life's problems; they are disappointed when he asks them to work on themselves and doesn't give them a mantra, which when chanted, would make their misfortunes disappear.

The most amazing thing is that the great mystic who heals and grants wishes in the blink of an eye is, at heart, a very hardworking and practical saint. He has always taken the long route, slow and steady like the turtle's (the large-eared rabbit of short cuts isn't his style). His way is the way of hard work and persistence. That's what pulls people to him. Even the lazy and crazy ones like me.

In all the time that I have worked on improving my mental and spiritual state, I have realized that we must create our own discipline. It is a gateway to heaven—a small paradise where you roam every day to gaze at the swaying grass, the flowing river and flying birds, your soul floating like a gentle breeze with the tides of time. Is there anything greater than to flow, to be at ease with yourself and with what life has dealt you? This enjoyment of our own company is the ultimate outcome of discipline.

It is when you start to look for ways to make time to be with yourself, with your practice or art, to dance barefoot in a different reality where your mind and heart are one, that you begin to grow spiritually, from a dithering sapling to a strapping young tree.

There is no confusion or conflict then; you are happy learning a new skill, craft or practice or honing an old one. Your discipline becomes your guardian of peace and composure. Is it any surprise then that the famous proverb,

'Work is worship,' is found in different tongues and dialects around the world, that work is considered a service to God?

If you are truly tired of your life, the way I was, and wish to turn it around, then you will need a discipline that nurtures your withering mind. Just as this body needs not just food, but nutritious food to stay fit and disease-free, our mental health depends upon the quality of our spiritual and worldly practices. Just working isn't enough, it will have to become a divine offering.

In the last couple of years, I have shared my spiritual practice with people from different age groups. Their experience of adopting this simple yet powerful discipline has been phenomenal. A great degree of sanity and peace has seeped into their minds. What motivated me to share the structure of my spiritual practice was my own success at having great order and quietude in my daily life. It is my most favourite thing in the world—my unwavering, unfailing prayer routine, 365 days a year. There are three steps to my daily spiritual practice:

1. **The Divine Song:**
    Every day in the last three-and-a-half years, after my morning bath, I sit down to eulogize God with the same devotional hymn (the Sri Hari arti).

2. **The Beautiful Quietude:**
    This is followed by a practice of *japa* and a light visualization to spend time with my deity, which allows me to experience great bliss and silence of the mind.

3.   **The Chit-Chat Afterwards:**
   It is in this sacred space that I admit to my failures, take stock of them and figure out better ways to lead my life.

I spend a beautiful hour daily in connecting with my higher self. It ushers in a rare clarity of mind that is incomparable to any worldly joy. The spirit, rejuvenated from moments spent in quietude, is then ready to face the real world with great peace and kindness. There is a confidence that stems from being under the spiritual shower of grace; you are soaked to the skin in bliss and focus. Life feels fuller, situations and people less intimidating and struggles feel like dead leaves that the soft breeze will surely blow away.

This practice might seem too simple, especially to those who have equanimity and balance in their lives, but to the one who is drowning or drifting in a strong current, it is no less than a life-saving raft to the rescue. A life of discipline is a life of fulfilment and ease.

However, sound mental and emotional well-being can never be complete without the discipline of physical exercise. A great tip to enhance our mental and physical health is a regular discipline of exercise. Its benefits are well known. Allow me to bring them to your attention anyway.

- Exercise is an effective, natural stress-buster. It is Nature's wonder drug, a natural painkiller, inbuilt in our body to combat stress.

- It flushes toxins like anxiety, fatigue and depression out of our system. When we get our body moving and blood flowing, our brain's hypothalamus and pituitary glands secrete neurochemicals called endorphins that help to generate feelings of euphoria and well-being.
- Endorphins light up the 'reward' circuit of our brain, which is typically related to pleasurable activities such as eating, drinking and being together. All the research on the benefits of exercising regularly come to the same conclusion.
- The chemicals or neurotransmitters like serotonin or norepinephrine released during exercise make us feel good naturally.

Cardio workouts are known to pull up dipping energy levels. A little exercise goes a long way in infusing a feeling of well-being in our daily life. I've been going for my evening run for over a decade now. A stretch of 22-25 minutes, five days a week, is all one needs to keep healthy, wealthy and wise. Well, even if we get one of them right by sweating it out, it is totally worth it!

Like everyone else, I used to enjoy taking a break from my exercise regime on Sundays and relax at home. Come Sunday evening, I would start thinking, 'People like to enjoy on Sunday, have some fun; hell, I should get some too.' And the next instant, I would be putting on my running shoes, because that is my relaxation and fun activity. It's like popping a feel-good pill without the side effects.

The addictive nature of exercise is undeniable, and there is an unfailing science behind why one gets hooked to it. The simple act of getting some alone time during exercise helps a person to regroup and think. It is a meditative activity. It makes you feel good, even when done for small windows of time.

No matter which age group you are in, how fit or unfit, slim or obese, if you start a routine of daily exercise, you are bound to increase your stamina and experience a great shift in your mental well-being. No couch potato has ever won a marathon.

The melancholy that often surrounds middle-aged and aged people is to a great degree the result of inactivity and overindulgence in unhealthy foods.

My guru, a great believer in exercise himself, gives great practical advice to people who come to him with their health problems: 'If you have 30 minutes in the morning, I suggest you meditate for 10 and exercise for 20 minutes. A fit body is far likely to house a fitter mind.'

A cool guru, isn't he? The coolest, I say.

Swamiji exercises four days a week for an hour in his personal gym. He believes the best minds can go to waste in the absence of physical activity. Human bodies are designed for moderate to intense physical labour, in the absence of which both the mind and body start to degenerate.

Let's remember that our mind is like a huge palace with multiple entry points. It can be seized by the enemy through any of these gates. Unless we deploy all our military resources and knowledge to safeguard it, we will always be under fire from the enemy, who wears the many hats of stress, fatigue, depression, anxiety and melancholy.

The more productive and disciplined our daily routine, the more meaningful our lives will feel.

The sanity of our lives depends heavily on the sanity of our daily routine. Stability and happiness come from having an unfailing discipline in life.

Be madly self-disciplined.

5
Time on earth

Have you ever loved someone so deeply that you have lived a long time in the fear of being separated from them in death one day? In time, that fear does come true. Death is the ultimate loss.

For thirteen years
I knew your face
I knew your smell
I knew your taste

You played with me
when no one was willing to
Your smiling eyes
could always make me smile

It's early day now
your memories so sweet
burn a hole
in my heart

Oh, such emptiness
I know not how to fill
I wish to raise a toast
treacherous tears spill

I loved you so
not parents
not lovers
could come so close

To hold you in my arms
So beautiful
so, calm
your greed, your innocence

One day I too will
leave everything behind
and find us a new home
eternal, inseparable

I lost Benoo, my black Labrador, a week after I celebrated my second year of renunciation. We had been together for 13 of the most stressful years of my life. Just as a firecracker lights up the sky, she lit up my morbid life with her wagging tail and cocky ears. She meant the world to me. I cannot explain my loss in better words than these—when I lost my mother, I had thought, 'Mamma had to go, and it's alright; she was ill and unhappy. But I have Benoo, and I'll be fine.'

Parting with Benoo wasn't easy. She was gone from the house like she had never been there. Her lovely memories lingered though; I was haunted by her tricks and her playfulness. The initial days of loss and emptiness were long and lonely. Minutes stretched like hours in mourning. It felt as if the grief would never end. Days heavy with sorrow weighed like boulders in my path. Yet, the beauty of existence is such that time does pass, and life goes on. The days no longer dragged; time, which had seemed bent out of shape, assumed its original carefree form. Had time changed, or had I?

Thanks to the detachment of a renunciate and the faith of a disciple in her guru, the pain soon dissipated into a fond remembrance of her. Yet, the very thought of those long, dreary days that followed her death still makes me shudder.

A couple of weeks after her demise, I was missing Benoo, and I said to Swamiji with utmost seriousness, 'You can do anything, Swamiji. Please, can you not make my time on earth go faster, so that I can be reunited with Benoo sooner?'

He answered gravely, albeit with a smile, 'Time is relative, Sadhviji. You stay joyous and it'll fly faster than you know.'

'What does it really mean, Swamiji, that time is relative?' I had read this in spiritual and self-help books of famous authors on quantum physics a long time ago, but I had little understanding of the subject.

'Your frame of mind will make your time on earth move rapidly for you. See, for so many people, the days seem long and dreary. And here you are, smiling merrily, enjoying your day. Life feels good, doesn't it?'

My mind was quick to remember the initial days of loss and emptiness after Benoo's demise. They were long and lonely. Minutes had stretched like hours; it felt as if time was crawling through the day. Not too surprisingly, just as my mind had shifted gears into an accepting phase, time had gained its lost momentum.

I had witnessed this over and over—during moments of mental agony and anguish, time did have a habit of slowing down. And the same time, in my everyday life, had a way of zipping past me. It was the strangest phenomenon I had ever encountered.

Belatedly, I realized I was gaping. I asked him again, 'So, all I need to do is stay happy and have fun, and time will pass quickly for me?'

'As Pliny the Younger, a Roman philosopher, has said, *"The happier the moments, the shorter the time."*'

'Is it really that simple, Swamiji?'

'There's a popular quote by Einstein, *"Put your hand on a hot stove for a minute, and it seems like an hour. Sit with a pretty girl for an hour, and it seems like a minute. That's relativity."* That's the long and short of it, Sadhviji.'

This exchange with Swamiji made me think that there was actually a way of cheating time. You could beat your time on earth not by moping or brooding over issues but by staying happy. What a beautiful thing it is! I could no longer wait to cheat time. I promised myself that I would live and laugh merrily, so that my time on earth would be over before I knew it. And six days in a week, I almost keep my promise.

Every day, the time we experience depends upon what we do and on our mood. The higher on energy we are, the faster time seems to pass. If you were to think of a task or a chore that you loathe, time seems to go on forever. On the other hand, when you pursue a hobby that you really enjoy, you are immersed in it and all of a sudden, the day has gone by. Time is an illusion. We can choose to accelerate our time on earth and be happy in the bargain.

If you were to take a hard look at your life, you would realize that no matter how challenging your circumstances, it was your outlook that determined the quality of your experience. A life of happiness and gratitude is far superior to a life of misery and complaint, for in both states of mind, time moves differently. It is like a pregnant woman being given a choice between a normal delivery and a C-section. She has to deliver the child anyway, but life is giving her an opportunity to deliver it the easier, more natural, healthier way.

In the early days of my *sannyasa*, when I would sit down for my *nitya karma* (daily *japa*), I would rush through the rounds of a rosary bead. It was just an item that I needed to tick off, so I could get on with my day. Those 20 minutes felt like an hour. Time moved as slowly as a snail, magnifying every ache and itch in the body. Sitting still seemed like the hardest thing in the world, and the mind kept flitting about like a fly. It was the same story every day. Some days were better than others, when I would lose myself in the *japa* for a few moments. But it lasted for not more than a few minutes, and then it was back to monkeying around until the time got over.

A year later, the scenario was quite different. An hour of *japa* began to feel more like 25 blissful minutes that had flown in the blink of an eye. Was it merely right practice on my part, or was it because I had now learnt to enjoy this activity, to find joy and bliss in it; therefore, the same time had changed its pace for me?

Everything that we experience is just a series of present moments. When lived right, they take away the despondency from our lives. We don't have to live in constant stress and anxiety when we can live a life of meaning by following a certain discipline, an inspiring ideology, cause or person, anything that makes us less self-centred and self-gratifying.

It is a unique perspective on life that we aren't exactly at the mercy of events beyond our control; we can choose to respond in a positive, upbeat and cheerful manner. A life of merriment is a short life, while a life of sadness is a never-ending road. Which one would you like to walk down? Why not play with time, befriend it, so that it may pass like a gently flowing river, carrying us through different landscapes of life to our union with the Divine ocean? Let us learn to be merry, and in that merriment, unlock and unravel the secret of time. Swamiji would always say to me, 'If we have to live, we might as well live gratefully and gracefully.'

Slow is my learning
slow
are its rewards, yet
what sweetness
is mixed

in the slowness
of this churning.

Slow
is my universe
separate
from time.

Gracefully manage your time on earth.

Sadhvi Vrinda with her beautiful Black Lab, Benoo

6
Train the dragon

Once, Swamiji scolded me for my misgivings and wrote this line in his e-mail:

'May Ma Jagdamba clear the garbage from your head.'

It was unusual because he rarely chastised me harshly, so much so that Swami Vidyananda had teasingly named me 'Bhakta Prahlad', the only one who could calm Narasimha *Bhagwan* in His Rudra avatar. On the rare occasions when Swamiji took on the Narasimha *swaroopa*, and everyone was reluctant to approach him, Swami Vidyananda would always nudge me to speak to our guru. Just as little children scuttle about the house watching out for an irate parent, Swami Vidyananda would put his hands up saying, 'You go and ask Swamiji if we should bring in his meal. In his current mood, I'm not going in.'

'What if he scolds me?' I would wail.

'Oh, he never scolds you. You are his Bhakta Prahlad,' he would finish teasingly.

It sounds very flattering, but the truth is that when Swamiji is in that quiet space, just a lift of his brow is enough to have you rooted to the spot. And yet, in all these years, Swamiji had been very kind to me. There is a simple but powerful reason behind this. He said to me many years ago, 'I never forget, even for a moment, Sadhviji, that you have no parents, that I am your parent. And I am your everything.'

That night, when I reread that line, 'May Ma Jagdamba clear the garbage from your head,' I cried like a child whose mother had left her to her own devices. For the next few hours, I didn't know what to do with myself. His approval meant everything to me. This new life, new name, new robe were all his gifts. In that moment, I wanted to die, for he had stated the truth—my head was truly filled with garbage. As I looked at the inner workings of my mind, I felt great repulsion for my small, constrained and resentment-seeped thinking. If there was any way of distancing oneself from oneself, I would have done it.

But the mind is the body, and the body is the mind. They are inseparable. There is no escaping them.

I barely slept that night. I remembered how I had come to the ashram five years ago, and what an arduous journey it had been to discard my old self and become this new person, this Sadhvi. It was like being flung back to the starting point when you thought you were nearing the finish line. I had failed miserably as a disciple and a person of God; I had gone back to being Dolly, the person I was before. I was finished. It may not appear much to you, the reader, but that's all I had to cling to, a better me. And in the absence of a better me, I didn't want to live. I wanted my guru to be proud of me, and I had achieved just the opposite.

Slowly, as the night passed and the flow of tears abated, some clarity began to appear on the horizon. Had I failed completely? Maybe not. Was I not beginning to make headway in my sadhana? There were times during my *japa* when I could see people's faces—someone in need, someone who was sad, someone going through a tough phase in life, someone I could help. My abilities were gradually growing to a degree where I could somehow gauge what people were going through and what help they sought from me. Their amazement at the accuracy of my reading surprised me as much as it surprised them.

These abilities—to accurately see, gauge and guide people—wouldn't have grown if divine grace had not been upon me, wasn't it? You don't become intuitive, perceptive and sagacious overnight; so, I must be doing something right. What was I missing then?

I knew that my intention wasn't a problem; it was my thinking. I had, since being under Swamiji's gentle shade, only become a kinder, gentler person. My intentions were always to be of use; I was indeed helping those who needed assistance, whether financial, spiritual or otherwise. How could I not want to help, when my guru was the epitome of altruism and unflinching kindness? I simply tried to emulate him. My heart was in the right place. And that brought me to an important question, *'If my heart was in the right place, and my intentions were pure, then why did my mind think the way it did?'*

Why did it cloud my judgement with negativity?

Why was I thinking what I was thinking, despite knowing that it was counterproductive to my spiritual growth?

Why was the same mind that was helping me scale new heights of consciousness being my worst enemy?

How could I break this cycle of Jekyll and Hyde?

I had heard Swamiji says a million times that if we have to break an old habit, we need to replace it with a new one. For every habit and every shortcoming that I had tried to overcome in the past, my mind had attacked me like a dragon spitting fire. The humbler I tried to be, the more egoistic I became. The gentler I tried to be, the angrier I got. It was as if my mind came fitted with an A-class inbuilt self-destructive mechanism that was set to blow up each time I tried to accomplish something good or noble. The freer I tried to be of my mind's controlling, negating ways, the more unbalanced I would become.

That morning, desperate to change, to win and earn my place back, I decided to take a *sankalpa* for 40 days. These were desperate times, and I was willing to put in a herculean effort.

In a moment of great calm, I took the following vow:

1. *I would vigilantly monitor my mind for thoughts that were negative or had a negative connotation.*
2. *I would discard every thought that was not conducive to my spiritual growth.*

These two parameters became the stringent guidelines based on which I started living out my days. I monitored every thought that popped into my head to see if it was conducive to my spiritual growth. If a thought had even the slightest negative connotation, I abandoned it and distracted myself by thinking of my spiritual practices, *Bhagwan* or anything pleasant that strengthened my resolve.

I didn't want to call this a practice in mindfulness just yet.

Back then, mindfulness was only a word. Even though I had edited and been a part of *Mind Full to Mindful,* a beautiful book by Swamiji, I had little practice at being mindful. Somewhere, I also had this faith that when Swamiji asks Ma Jagdamba for something, it always comes to fruition. He had given me a blessing and it had come to pass, as all other words uttered by Swamiji came true. With a strong belief in my guru's power and might, I began my *sankalpa* of monitoring my mind for negative thoughts. Over a period of time, I developed an organized system, a technique that I chose to call the **Train-It Model.**

THE TRAIN-IT MODEL

My Train-It model had a three-level commitment on my part, a commitment that was as vital to me as breathing air. It became my single point of focus every day for 40 days. Everything else became secondary—my sadhana, *japa*, prayer. Everything else in life ceased to hold any significance except the determination to see this through. This commitment to train my mind became my only living, breathing, walking and talking prayer. A prayer that I soon realized wasn't easy to live by.

Here is my journey of those early days.

Watch-It

The first important thing was to start watching my mind the moment my day began. It seemed easy at first to see what the mind was thinking, but often, during the day, the mind would just suck me into black holes. A train of thought would have gone really far before I realized that I was thinking what I was thinking. This senseless thinking (compare it to senselessly flicking TV channels without really knowing what to watch) was what was really damaging the mind, muddying the water and kicking up all that dirt.

I consciously began to stop myself from chasing diverse thoughts. Since my actions and speech were directly impacted by my thoughts, I became more vigilant about the quality of the thoughts that arose in my mind. Though the intensity and frequency of negative thoughts dwindled with time, I still had to face a handful of persistent, lingering, anxiety-filled, stress-ridden and disturbing thoughts.

We all have this relationship with certain issues in our life. They are a rotting, decaying but inseparable part of ourselves.

Many times a day, I would flow with my thoughts, deeply enmeshed in them, until it was too late to retreat from the gloom they were creating. The challenge was to prevent the mind from revisiting them at every opportunity, like a man seeking out his paramour.

Feed-It

The solution came to me in the guise of a beautiful rendition of *Devi Bhagavatam* by Ramesh Menon. The more I read about the glories of the Devi and rejoiced, the more at ease my mind felt. In quiet moments, when negative thoughts lurked in the corners of my mind, I would quickly switch my attention to the stories I had been reading.

I realized that to distract myself from a barrage of negative thoughts, I had to equip myself with good-quality content on a daily basis, at least in the beginning.

I began feeding my mind inspiring quotes from my guru and his writings, devotional hymns and interesting news pieces. The more I exposed my mind to inspirational literature, diverse ideas and new perspectives, the more material my mind had to process. Feeding my mind a dose of quality and prayerful thoughts went a long way in distracting it from negative thoughts. This conscious feeding, reading and contemplation became the determining factor in winning against my powerful mind's gigantic storehouse of bad memories and horseshit.

Filter-It

Despite the strict vigilance and quality input, there were times when my mind would run rampant like a bull on the loose. On some days, no matter how hard I tried, I just couldn't stop my mind from being sad, negative, unhappy or angry. I would feel like a loser, helpless and at the mercy of my raging emotions. What more could I do? I began to take stock of the situation at the end of every day, monitoring my progress on how I had fared that day.

Soon, my mind started to identify triggers, situations and reactions that made me feel sad or angry. It started to know how certain responses, people or events might make me feel. This knowledge was gold, for my mind could now anticipate potentially risky situations and either steer clear of them, or come up with pre-decided responses that would help me cope better.

During my *sankalpa* of monitoring my thoughts for negativity and discarding thoughts that were not conducive to my spiritual growth, I adopted the following practice at the end of the first day. I mentally picked out the thoughts that I couldn't thwart and which went on to become full-fledged terrorists because I had failed to nip them in the bud.

As I continued to filter and monitor my thoughts each day and recap them at night, my mind slowly began to recognize potentially damaging thoughts the moment they began to arise. I could dismiss them with the flick of a finger most of the time, but sometimes, they overpowered me with an intensity that nearly broke my *sankalpa*.

On the 14th day, I suffered my biggest setback—not only was my mind swimming in negativity, but I also ended up acting upon my thoughts. This double impact of negative thought and action derailed me completely. My vow was little more than an obscure obituary in a poorly circulated newspaper. I failed to keep my mind free of negativity for over two days. On the third day, some semblance of normalcy began to return, but the damage to my confidence and self-esteem had already been done.

I had two choices: I could abandon the *sankalpa* or see it through. I chose to see it through. Once again, I mustered all my courage and enthusiasm and got back to monitoring my mind, carefully watching out for past triggers or potential incidents that could upset my balance. I resumed my practice exactly from where I had left off. I was like a woman crazed, guarding the fortress of my mind like a valiant queen. The blow had come as a blessing in disguise, for I became even more adamant to win.

And then it started to happen. Every day, little by little, I became more and more mindful of what I was thinking. It was a slow process and a painful one in many ways. But I became better at picking out productive thoughts from noisy, senseless ones. I learnt to safeguard my mind and its peace from unfriendly invaders by simply not letting them in.

One morning, I woke up at around 4 am, still groggy and dull with sleep, when to my greatest surprise, the other half of my mind was already mulling deeply over some unkind thoughts. My mind had not even fully awakened, and yet, a part of it was already ruminating on negative events. I hadn't done the thinking; I had been merrily sleeping. Then who was really thinking all these negative thoughts?

I realized then how much garbage each one of us is carrying in the mind, from situations, conversations, incidents and tragedies that happen to us and around us every day. The mind keeps processing and throwing it all up on the pristine shore of our consciousness, polluting it. Like clueless idiots, we think about things that we don't wish to think about, playing the same old tape, making similar mistakes and then wondering why we are unhappy or discontented. Does it all not stem from the mind?

And so, I learnt the most important lesson of my life:

There is nothing greatly wrong with me or my life, or most people's lives. We have all just been living with an untrained and untamed mind, conditioned to be unhappy.

The mind has known negativity, pessimism and un-happiness for so long that it keeps returning to this familiar territory of its own accord. Unless we train the mind to change its perspective, it will continue to drag us down. Despite our best efforts, it will continue to behave irrationally.

Two things, however, will act as your biggest barriers in taming the mind. Watch out for these imposters along the way.

Guilt

The lingering ghosts of the past and mistakes of the present are seldom easy to shake off. Follies, failures and inaction give rise to feelings of acute remorse, regret and even shame. The golden rule when walking on the path of self-purification is to keep going, even when you fail or fall. A guilt-ridden mind will only slow us down. Before we begin to train our mind, we must be clear that there will be disappointments and mistakes along the way. We must face them bravely and march ahead.

Insecurity

The seed of insecurity, in most people, is sown quite young. In my experience, the more stability you have been exposed to in the formative years of your life, the more secure and fearless you will feel as a grown-up. A childhood marked by a dysfunctional family, a troubled parent or unrestful circumstances has a deep impact on our psyche. The security and safety that have been elusive in a child's life are hardly likely to manifest in adulthood.

To deal with the things that make you insecure, examine them one by one and discuss them with a parent, a partner, or a person who gives rise to these feelings of insecurity in you. Talking about your insecurity is like wiping away the layer of dust that has been gathering on an unused gadget.

Stare at your insecurity hard and long, and remember that one day, we are all going to die; so, is it really worth holding on to this harrowing feeling of anxiety and constant fear? Analyze it and come up with your antidote to feeling less alone. The answer must lie somewhere in you.

As far as I can recall, I have been mostly an insecure person. I have either failed everyone I have ever loved—that's what I feel—or I have been separated from them. My insecurity does not allow me to feel happy or free for long periods of time.

It wants to cling to the other person and make unacceptable demands on their time and space. The more I wish to mould myself in their mould, the more troubled and sorrowful I feel. It is as if this restlessness is in my blood. Sometimes, it disappears for months altogether, giving me hope, only to be triggered out of the blue by an innocuous event.

Have I come up with a way to deal with it? Well, I have. But sometimes nothing works. And just admitting this fact that sometimes nothing will work and we will find ourselves in the grip of a feverish insecurity, helps put things in perspective. It calms me as I gather my strength one day at a time, to banish it again from my consciousness and return to my old, carefree routine. 'Don't give up' is the only mantra that works sometimes, combined with being patient with our own conniving self.

THE ONE TRUTH

After my first *sankalpa*, I went on to take many more, and I failed just as many. My mind, which was now habituated to taking *sankalpas* to purify my thoughts, speech and action, began to infuse and tweak my Train-It practice to be more positive, efficient and competent.

Should you choose to practise this technique, you will notice that the mind starts to believe in itself once you have completed two or three *sankalpas*. The science behind it is quite simple—any activity that you diligently follow for 40 days becomes a habit. Imagine the peace and power of a mind that is habituated to remain positive and pure, striving towards a higher goal in life.

Incidentally, in January 2019, just as I was glancing through the final draft of this manuscript before submitting it to our publishers, I came across the very first post written by Swamiji in June 2011. It was penned barely a month after his inexplicable vision of Lord Narayana and was originally an e-mail, apprising his near and dear ones of his well-being after a gap of nearly one-and-a-half years. In the e-mail, Swamiji had shared the truth as he had discovered it during his arduous journey of self-realization.

Even though I must have read that post a couple of times over the last few years, like the many things we know, read, marvel at and forget, I had no recollection of its contents. Until that night, when I sat agape at my desk thinking, 'Oh, I made a similar discovery!' My path was a shabby, poor shadow of my guru's glorious, laborious, path of self-realization. I was a bumbling panda, while he was the unequivocal Master Oogway of the Valley of Peace, and yet, our paths collided.

This excerpt (used with permission) from Swamiji's maiden post on the blog was an eye-opener for me. All the lame effort I had been putting in had got me to the same realization, the same One Truth.

Self-realization is no serendipity. It is not an 'Aha!' moment. Intellectual comprehension of such realization may well be an epiphany; the actual realization is far from it. Self-realization can be achieved by anyone who is willing to put in the effort. The dawning of such realization will leave you with only answers. You will no longer have any questions. Intellectually, you may understand the underlying philosophy or doctrinal principles, but such an understanding may only make you more rigid. You will end up merely subscribing to a theory with no confirmation about its validity.

If you believe that the Divine has a form, you can see His form in this very lifetime. If you believe that the Divine is formless, you can experience deep absorption (samadhi) in the foreseeable future. That is what I experienced multiple times. Your world is made up of your thoughts. If your world has a God in it and all your thoughts, all the time, are about Him, His very form will manifest before you. If your world has bliss and all your thoughts, all the time, are focused on such bliss, you will experience such bliss. That is a tough task though, because a perfectly stable and still mind is required to meditate on one thought for prolonged periods. It can be achieved with an initial intense effort.

The truth is very simple, and you all know it too. But experiencing it is an entirely different ballgame. Most people know right from wrong, yet why do they find themselves engaging in unscrupulous and undesirable acts repeatedly?

That is because their mind is not tamed. A restless mind and its modifications (citta vritti) drive them towards experiencing and enjoying the world through their body alone. Purity of discipline, whether in bhakti or in dhyana, can help you tame your mind.

You will then experience an indescribable, incessant flow of bliss. I used to read about it and had some experiences, far and few in between. The actual sustained experience of samadhi is an incredible one. The bliss stays with you all the time with very little effort afterwards.

I would like to elucidate the difference between intellectual comprehension of the truth and actually experiencing it. Suppose that someone is suffering from cataract. That person is aware of his visual impairment. Is that awareness adequate to correct his vision? He knows where the problem is, and he knows that the resultant effect is his inability to see correctly. He is also aware that undergoing a procedure to remove the cataract will fix his vision. Intellectually, he gets it. He understands it. That awareness does not help him in seeing unhindered though. His impairment is not the result of any intellectual malfunction. Therefore, it cannot be fixed with any intellectual comprehension or correction. He must undergo the procedure to correct his vision. Similarly, your distorted view of the world or your deluded mind (citta) is not an intellectual problem.

Subscribing to any philosophy or believing a certain theory to be the truth—both of which are functions of the mind—is not going to help you uncover your true self, let alone any samadhi or darshan of your deity. The most beautiful thing is that you can experience your true nature and you can experience that incessant flow of bliss by taming your mind.

A mind that is not settled and under complete control will render you unable to perform devotional service (bhakti) or meditation (dhyana) correctly and purely.

These lines resonated with me, for I had been trying to accomplish this for too long. These words renewed my faith in my practice. I couldn't hope for something as divine as self-realization—it was for the extraordinary hearts like my guru's—but what I could hope for was self-purification through the training of my mind. The Train-It model wasn't just a lame attempt on my part to cope; it was indeed the way forward.

I felt wise beyond my years. Over-eager to share the knowledge of my practice with others, I said to Swamiji, 'It's such an effective practice. Everyone could train their mind with the Train-It technique, Swamiji, couldn't they?'

Smiling at my eagerness to share my learning with the world, Swamiji replied, 'It is easy for you because you are relentless in your drive to purify yourself. It is this unyielding, undying perseverance that is needed to break the set tendencies of the mind.'

This is the highest compliment my guru has bestowed upon me. It felt like someone was pouring honey in my ears. I could have squealed with happiness, but I maintained my composure. I was, after all, learning to be a calm and equanimous sannyasi.

To cut a long chapter short, to achieve the extraordinary, all an ordinary human being needs is to start training and taming the mind relentlessly. It is why the power of a *sankalpa*, a vow, is unmatchable.

To control the mind, to prevent this powerful machine from reducing you into a puppet in its hands, you need to simply *Train-It*.

1. **Watch-It:** Filter your thoughts.
2. **Feed-It:** Follow a deliberate practice of reading, listening to and speaking good, inspirational material.
3. **Filter-It:** Constantly question what you are thinking.

The shortest path to self-improvement is self-purification, says my guru.

Tame the dragon, *Train-It*.

7
The power of kindness

The flames from the fire leapt into the dark night. Dark faces, curious eyes, small bodies smiled into the bonfire. The faces illuminated by the red glow of the burning fire were anything but unhappy. They seemed merry except for a baby who kept crying into the night, clinging to his mother's chest. The woman, Chandani, barefoot, clad in a shabby cotton sari, sat at the edge of the circle of little children and two men. Standing by the large glass window of my puja-room-cum-study, I watched them laugh and shout. The flames, bright and high, cast a beautiful reflection on my glass window six stories up. I could only watch them, mesmerized.

A trail of a road ran into a few abandoned plots in front of my apartment complex; a labourer couple and their siblings had recently settled on that land. It was almost like they had disembarked from the general compartment of a train and landed here without any luggage or belongings. I watched them a little enviously as they laughed and joked and fought. They didn't have much, but they had each other. While I stood on the other side, cosy but alone, with the air-conditioning that blew hot air in my room. Alone with my thoughts, with my struggling, unhappy self.

It was the beginning of 2017, Makar Sankranti to be precise, and I had taken a 21-day vow of silence. It was yet another attempt to be free of my diseased mind. I had been a renunciate for a little over six months by then. In silence, I ate my dinner, still watching them.

A light drizzle had started to fall, and I saw the fire outside die down to smouldering embers. One by one, the small children began to crawl into a makeshift tent. Some wore sweaters; others didn't. The biting cold outside couldn't care less whether or not the children were protected against it.

Every few minutes, the screen of a mobile phone shone some light inside the tent, and I would get a glimpse of small children, aged 3 to 13 years, their angular arms and legs lying across each other's. The grown-ups also lay side by side. In all, 13 people, most of them children, lay in that small tent, shivering in the cold.

It was 9 pm. I contemplated going down that otherwise empty road. My vow of silence prohibited me from having any kind of communication; still, I picked up my phone and called Bhupen, Deepa's husband; their loving family took care of me in this bustling city.

I let the phone ring to let him know I needed something. Soon, Ashu, Bhupen's mischievous daughter, came upstairs to find out what I needed. I handed Ashu a pink quilt and a bag full of warm clothes (whatever I could lay my hands on was packed into that bag) for the children and pointed to the dying fire outside. When she could make no sense of my gestures, I wrote down a note for Bhupen, asking him to go right away and give the quilt and woollens to the children. We also added some biscuits and chips.

Five minutes later, I watched Bhupen, a tall, lone figure, walking towards the tent. Bhupen had been running these errands of kindness for me for a long time. Whether I saw a hungry puppy from my window or a lone vegetable-seller in need, the first person I called was Bhupen, for I knew his heart was just as kind and keen on helping others.

As soon as the little ruffians heard Bhupen's voice, they crawled out to see what other promises the night held for them. Like a spirit watching from heaven, I watched the children gathered around him, opening a pack of biscuits, a bag of chips. I went to bed a lot more elated than I had felt since my silence practice had started. I had been living in this dragging quietude for 10 days.

In the morning, when I woke up, the first thing I saw was the pink quilt covering the children. They slept peacefully, like the fresh litter of a stray huddled together. That morning, even the sun streaming in through my window could not match my bright smile or demeanour. I felt useful. I felt as if I had done my duty. Even if I had had to break my vow of silence the previous evening, I would have done so to keep those children warm. I was a renunciate eager to help the society I lived in. It is what my guru had said to me at the time of my *deeksha*, 'You are a sannyasi from today. Go and serve the world and give up your life in service.'

I had wondered then of what service I could be to the world. I was eager to give up my life but that was more out of a sense of hopelessness than anything else. But, one thing I knew that the quickest way to feel good about myself was to do something selfless, but where could I find people to feed or clothe every day? It wasn't feasible on a daily basis, or was it?

The more I did for others, the stronger I felt. And truly, what was the point of accumulating all that clarity of mind and wisdom, if I wasn't going to apply it to the welfare of people around me? If you choose to walk this path, with your newly gained perspective you will find yourself asking at some point, 'How can I be of use to others?'

As a child, I always saw my father pull out no less than a fifty- or hundred-rupee note, whenever someone approached him for alms.

'Ashok, just give them five or ten rupees. Don't give them so much...' Mamma used to chide him.

'My principle is quite simple,' Papa had replied gently on one of those occasions, stroking his moustache, 'If someone comes to me and says he's hungry, I want to make sure that he doesn't go begging around before he can buy a decent meal.' Papa always looks so dashing in his uniform, I had thought.

'Their needs are endless.'

'So are God's resources, Rita.'

Such is the power of kindness that both the giver and the receiver feel rewarded. This became the next big step on my spiritual journey, 'How can I be kinder?' Now that my mind functioned at a greater capacity, with clear skies becoming more frequent than overcast days, I felt capable of handling larger issues of existence. Even though I was still a work-in-progress, I had enough clarity and calm to find solutions to other people's problems, both practically and transcendentally.

It is this faith Swamiji had invested in me that someday, I would wake up from my selfish stupor and realize that my true happiness lay in the happiness of others. And that one day, service to mankind was truly going to set me free. It was going to define my present and my future. The new mindset helped me see many possibilities and opportunities every day to be selfless in my pursuit of serving others. With the introduction of Rak (Random Acts of Kindness) on the Black Lotus App, founded by Swamiji, a whole new world of kindness and selfless service was thrown open.

He had created this app to revolutionize the world, flood it with kindness and so much goodness that people in every corner of the world could lead meaningful lives. His immense spiritual wealth attracted both talent and material wealth like a magnet, and Black Lotus was a living, breathing reality in a short span.

The most admirable trait about my mystical guru, one of the greatest Siddhas perhaps to walk this earth, with great healing powers running through his delicate hands, is that he has never resorted to supernatural powers to meet people's worldly needs. Instead, he works very hard to provide for those who look up to him. It is a well-known fact that Swamiji never takes any personal donations.

Meditation retreats and royalties from his books are his only sources of income, a negligible amount for someone from whose personal account over Rs 100,000 are auto-debited every month to support children's education, pensions to ageing couples and for expenses to run homes of families that have little or no financial support. Then there are the donations made anonymously to individuals and organizations. At the end of every financial year, he gives away all the excess in his account and starts all over again. No sane person does that. Not even for a moment am I calling this insanity; it is the highest form of detachment known only to a true yogi. Just like ants toil to gather food for the coming winter, Swamiji starts writing again to generate income, to nourish not just starving souls but bodies.

On one of his visits abroad, a single parent came to seek his blessings. Her only child, a three-year-old girl, suffered from a genetic condition that didn't allow her to swallow food without giving rise to complications in the small child's body. The child was born with a short food-pipe. The treatment and surgery for her condition weren't merely costly; it was also a great challenge for medical science to undertake such an operation. There were no guarantees that even if the surgery was successful, the body would adapt to the foreign element placed in it.

Swamiji was greatly moved by the child's situation. She looked like any other toddler of her age, except that she was fed through a pipe in her belly. He was greatly perturbed as well. Just as even the greatest surgeon cannot save every patient who comes to him, Swamiji wasn't sure if he could really help this child. That night, he went on to the website that the child's mother had created to raise funds for her surgery and made an anonymous contribution. You might wonder how I know about the donation if it was made anonymously.

Just like people in high positions in the corporate world, CEOs, MDs or honest policemen are unable to segregate their professional lives from their personal, Swamiji too has a tough time overcoming people's sorrows and pleas for help, long after the meetings are over. The more helpless the situation, the more vulnerable he feels for not being able to work his way around Mother Nature at times. That night, he had forwarded the website link, which had many beautiful pictures of a curly-haired child smiling in her mother's arms. The e-mail read:

I've been looking at the little girl's pictures for a while. I wish more could be done for her.

(The mother of that child was able to raise enough funds for the child's treatment. The child has recovered well and is now happy and healthy like other children of her age.)

After seeing Swamiji's life from such close quarters, I have arrived at the conclusion that while working on self-improvement is a prerequisite, kindness and service to others is the natural curve of the spiritual path. What is the point of making it through a jungle infested with zombies, when everyone else who was with you got eaten or left behind? While you may be floating in peace, you cannot ignore the poignant cries arising from your neighbour's home. We must stand up for the lost, the abandoned, the hurt and grieving, the poor and diseased, like my guru stands up for those who seek his divine umbrella.

And what is even more heartening is that the people Swamiji supports—financially and spiritually—will never really know how hard he works day and night so that they can lead better lives, their children can go to better schools and universities, old couples can gracefully lead retired lives and families can hold their heads high.

What can we ask of God, if we ourselves aren't willing to give to those who are in direr straits? If a moment of our life is of use to someone, then we have already marked ourselves present in the grand classroom of our merciful creator. I am forever inspired by my master's selfless service to the society.

Kindness is prayer.

The long road home

The reason for the title of this last chapter is that no one can really say with surety that they have arrived. You will cross many milestones, but the destination, though visible, will always remain a little out of grasp. Your heart will brim with pride when you look back at how far you have come and what you have left behind. At the same time, it will dread the daunting task of further purifying yourself. On this endless journey, your confidence will shatter like a piece of china a hundred times, each time more gruelling than the last. Days, months and years will not be enough; the long road home will truly be the longest road you have ever travelled. Moments of enlightenment, like a master's light touch on the forehead, will electrify you and pull you out of the dungeons of despair, only to throw you back far deeper the next time.

The bricks on the head will continue to rain unabated, but something beautiful will have started taking shape, a tiny sapling of humility and conviction unknown to man will have sprung in the heart. It will truly mark the advent of a remarkable journey, where you remain unfazed and untroubled by the past or present, free of guilt, free of the negativity that was once so ingrained in you. The purity of your thoughts, like a halo, will protect you from the world and from yourself.

Life's struggles, like standing rainwater on the terrace, won't just disappear overnight. But priceless treasures of contentment and tranquillity, and intuitive phenomena that can't really be explained, will start to appear in your life. Have you not noticed, how at the end of each day, when we lie in our beds, a sweet unawareness is waiting to engulf us, embrace us in its warm quilt of darkness and nothingness? Like an angel, sleep descends upon us, freeing us, untangling us from our lives for a wee bit, restoring balance in our mind and bodies. In the loving arms of the night, we heal; in sleep, we are restful and at peace.

At dawn, once again, we rise. We wake up to a promise of numerous opportunities to do good, be good or give in to our baser nature. Each day is a mix of challenges and struggles, laughter and anxiety, madness and fatigue, until the night comes to whisk them away.

Just as this never-ending cycle of day and night, work and rest, highs and lows is the basis of life, similarly, the path of self-improvement and self-purification is a constant cycle of ups and downs, learning and unlearning. No matter what an adept you become on this path, no one is exempt from the challenges that life will continue to put your way, until you breathe your last.

However, to give up on yourself midway through this path would be a shame, for untold, unlimited and heightened levels of consciousness lie ahead. A consciousness that is unafraid and tireless in the pursuit of others' welfare. An ever-present crystal clarity of thought, a new mindset, a new perspective and a new mind in the old body will soon manifest.

'This new perspective is everything,' says Swamiji, 'Buddha called it *vipashya*, insight.'

To attain this new perspective and scale its dizzy heights involves a long journey through gigantic glaciers of anger and ego, rivers of grief and greed, deep forests of lust and stupor, until you finally arrive at the gates of heaven—your pristine, unsullied, godly self. Of all the tasks a man may undertake, self-purification is the sole purpose of his birth. My master's life is the most humbling example of a man's union with the Divine. His unearthly persistence in meditating on the divine form of the Devi, to manifest Her as you and me, is indeed the most miraculous occurrence of our times.

One day, the world will wake up to the magnitude of it, perhaps after he's gone. But his life will continue to inspire people from all faiths to take this long road home, a perilous road of hard work, renouncement, divine love and truthfulness. These were mere words of a spoken language before Swamiji came and breathed them to life. I owe everything I have come to be, my very existence, to my great master. His mind is like a diamond mine, with brilliant stones of all shapes and sizes lying in plain sight, waiting to be brushed and gifted to anyone who holds out her palm.

I thank him for his extraordinary gift—the gift of a new way of thinking.

The great blessing

Even though I am a storyteller, while penning these hidden, painful, some forgotten and some fresh and reckless incidents from my life, I felt embarrassed and a tad reluctant, not knowing whether, as a reader, you would see my challenges as your challenges, or whether they would appear to you as yet another sob story of a lost girl. I was putting my life of so many years, bereft of any real achievements, out there for the scrutiny of people I would probably never meet. And yet, I felt brave and courageous for sharing, for unbeknownst to us, there are many like me, who are lost and directionless and are battling with their minds with no one to turn to or look up to.

I figured that I am nearing 40 anyway, and one day, I would disappear from the face of this earth like I never existed. What if someone could truly benefit from my mistakes and learn and evolve from my struggles? It was with this sentiment alone that I sought Sri Hari's refuge (the beautiful, resplendent, wish-fulfilling Lord of our temple and my heart) to grant me the wisdom to see this book through.

I am aware that what I have written may sound too altruistic to be true, but it is the truth. It is the only reason for the book's existence. These words have come about with my guru's grace alone.

Before I go, I want you to know that at times, despite putting your best out there, some will still not understand you or will misunderstand you. With some people, there will never be a level playing field.

Some friction, like a bad hair day, will always be a part of our lives. Just as you are going through your own journey, battling flaws and inner struggles, so are others. When they lash out, or are unreasonable and unkind, let it go; it's for your own peace of mind. Let not the purity of your new perspective be exposed to the blemishes of others' shortcomings.

We all are somewhere mirror images of each other. In this circle of life, you will do some good, and some will be done to you. You will do some bad, and that too will find its way back to you. In this transactional world, the only thing worth holding on to is His grace.

May Mother Divine purge and purify you, just as lovingly as She showed me the way out of the dark.

This book is the longest prayer I have ever made.

Unless you are willing to help yourself, no power in the three worlds can help you. Wake up to this truth now.

On that note, this little book comes to an end.

With the greatest love and reverence, I bow at my guru's divine feet. He truly is the scriptural personification of a guru in this day and age.

A billion *pranams*, Swamiji.

Afterword

From Om Swami

'Will you please write an afterword for my book?' Sadhvi Vrinda said to me one day.

'Don't people normally write the foreword for a book they recommend?'

'That's the whole point, Swamiji,' she said to me. 'I don't want people to read this book because you are recommending it. I just want some words from you as a blessing.'

'I will,' I said, and forgot all about it. Until now, when she emailed me the finished manuscript already typeset by the publisher, ready to roll. 'Please do not write any nice things about me,' she had said, 'just your thoughts on the book and blessings.'

It's not easy being a guru, every day you have to appear for some exam and come out with flying colours. Every time a follower's or disciple's belief is shaken, they question you. Those who look up to you have set views about how you should be; you are constantly judged by those around you. So, when I initiated Sadhvi Vrinda Om, three years ago, a million questions ran through many people's minds. They had their own ideas about what an ideal disciple should look like or what a sannyasi should be like, or why would I initiate someone directly into sannyasa and so on. Some directly and some otherwise bombarded me with coulda, woulda, shoulda and all that. But, even for a moment, indeed even for a fraction of a moment, I had no doubt that not just mine but the blessings of the entire lineage were with Sadhvi Vrinda.

And, the reason for that is quite simple: she's easily the most candid and honest person I have ever met in my life. The only other person whom I've seen to be so utterly truthful is my own father. Sadhvi Vrinda is not afraid to speak of her challenges and shortcomings. Yes, many do that in front of their guru, but few do that in front of the whole world. It does not just take courage but infinite truthfulness to do that. Most gurus and initiates, sannyasis or otherwise, quickly mount the pedestal and pretend to be above the vagaries of life. This is the first book I have read by a sannyasi that is so brutally honest. And it is Sadhviji's commitment to truth that is truly remarkable. It is what I saw and the masters in my lineage saw. No pretense, no cloaks, just someone who is willing to tell the truth.

As I say always, the truth may not sound fascinating at first but eventually it melts the listener and reaches home. That's what truth does. It is for that reason that I feel that her learnings and lessons in this book will help you see the world in a new way. It is up to us to be happy and do something beautiful with our lives, this book shows you how to do that in a practical and pragmatic manner. I'm certain every sincere reader will see the value in this work.

Yes, it's true that when all else fails, a prayer sees you through. You know why? Not because a prayer is a plea, but it's the ultimate expression of truth, surrender and devotion. What else one needs to turn one's life into a blessing? Nothing, I say.

The title could not have been more apt and the contents truer. Well done, Sadhviji. I am proud of you.

Peace.
Swami